The Whole Woman

The Whole Woman

Fashioned in His Image

by

Faye C. Stowe

Beacon Hill Press of Kansas City
Kansas City, Missouri

Printed in the
United States of America
ISBN: 0-8341-0913-1

Permission to quote from the following copyright versions is acknowledged with
sincere appreciation:

The Holy Bible, New International Version (NIV), copyright © 1978 by the
New York International Bible Society.

The Living Bible (TLB), © 1971 by Tyndale House Publishers, Wheaton, Ill.

(All quoted scriptures are taken from NIV
unless otherwise indicated.)

10 9 8 7 6

To Gene, my best friend, sweetheart, and husband.
His constant encouragement
made the writing of this book possible.

Contents

Acknowledgments

If there is any credit to be given for the writing of this book, may it be given to Christ. He has been my daily source of strength, inspiration, and guidance.

My heartfelt thanks to Betty Fuhrman and Fred Parker, super editors; to Mary Ann Wagner, super typist; to Cleo Fletcher, super friend, resource person, and prayer partner.

Preface

My first compulsion for writing this book came in response to some Christian women who voiced a sense of discouragement and frustration in their spiritual journey.

I have tried to assure them that they need not experience defeat or disappointment in feeling that they have not arrived—none of us have! God is continually working on each of us. We should never stop growing in the area of spiritual maturity; obedience and discipline; faith and compassion.

However, God *does* expect us to be at our best. And because we are fashioned in the image of Jesus we have the potential of realizing all of the attributes of His human personality. When He occupies the throne of sovereignty in our lives, our minds and spirits merge into a oneness of purpose with Him.

"I live; yet not I, but Christ
liveth in me" (Gal. 2:20, KJV).

His peace and strength become stronger within us than anything Satan can initiate.

We should be content with nothing less than achieving "wholeness." This will be contingent upon our functioning properly as God intended—spiritually, physically, and mentally. Only then will we excel in our spiritual aspirations and goals for Christian service.

Women, the world needs us—but more importantly, God needs us. He has created us unique and special on purpose. Let's celebrate our *specialness!* Let's infect others with our contagious Christianity.

Christ 'did some fashioning on me even during the writing of this book. My prayer is that He may do the same for you as you read it.

—Faye C. Stowe

SECTION I

The Whole Woman—Spiritually

1

Celebrating Christian Wholeness

Eve was a whole woman.

She was fashioned by God in His image—"God created man [and woman] in his own image, . . . male and female he created them" (Gen. 1:27).

And how was Eve like Him? "Holy" is used to describe God more than any other word in the Bible. Basically this means "whole" or "perfect." The Holy Spirit was housed in her heart. His presence made her a holy, whole person spiritually.

This wholeness also included her mind and body. She enjoyed perfect health. No germs or illness troubled her. The first days with her husband, Adam, in the Garden of Eden were literally "heaven on earth." Their communion with God as well as with each other was a beautiful demonstration of perfection in harmonious living.

The Bad News

Then something tragic happened. The first man and woman yielded to temptation and sinned. They lost their wholeness. One of the definitions of the word *whole* is "nothing taken away." The day Adam and Eve disobeyed God they suffered a grievous loss—several things were taken away!

1. Their Health

They would never again be the same spiritually, physically, or mentally. Sin brought sickness and death—"by the trespass of the one man, death reigned" (Rom. 5:17).

2. Their Happiness

The pain of childbirth suffered by women was an example of one of the many ways in which their lives would be cursed with tears and sorrow. A further penalty for their sin is recorded in Gen. 3:17, "Cursed is the ground because of you; through painful toil you will eat of it all the days of your life."

3. Their Harmony

Not only was their communion with God destroyed, but their communication with each other broke down as well. Each blamed the other for their sins. In just a few years one of their sons would quarrel with his brother and commit the first murder.

And this has been the pattern of our world ever since. Instead of being whole as God intended, we are unhealthy, unhappy, and unharmonious. This is the bad news!

The Good News

God did not leave humanity hopeless. The gospel literally means "Good News." Jesus came that we might have abundant life (John 10:10). His death at Calvary provided forgiveness for our sins (1 John 1:9) and cleansing from all unrighteousness (1 John 1:7).

He can make us whole women spiritually! We can be fashioned by God and enjoy the same perfection of wholeness with which Adam and Eve were created. As Bill Gaither's gospel song reminds us, God's touch makes us whole.

The word *holy* in the German language really means "health."

Holiness is spiritual health. The healing of full salvation has conquered the disease of sin in our hearts. Sins forgiven—sin cleansed—self-will crucified. The spirit is now healthy again.

Get Up and Grow

Just as healthy babies have to grow, so the born-again believers have a lot of growing to do—even Spirit-filled Christians.

Sometimes this is accomplished through the fires of adversity. Dresden china, the finest in the world, is burned three times. Why does it go through this intense fire? Once or twice should be enough! No, three times are necessary to burn this exquisite china so that the gold and crimson colors are brought out beautifully and permanently. So it is with us as Christian women.

Our trials are burned into us again and again. And by God's grace these lovely colors will be there and there to stay.

However, this perfect spiritual health does not mean perfect physical, mental, and emotional health. We are all still under the curse of death. Only the spirits of those who are "new creatures" in Christ have eternal life (2 Cor. 5:17). Our minds and bodies will die. But though Christians are not immune from physical disease and mental illness, the Lord wants us to enjoy the best health possible.

He wants our bodies, which are the temples in which the Holy Spirit resides, to be clean and strong (1 Cor. 6:19). He has also made provision for good mental hygiene so that our minds and emotions will be Christlike.

This spiritual, physical, and mental/emotional health harmonizes and integrates our whole being into a unified personality.

Christian Wholeness Is Something to Celebrate!

John Wesley taught that the holier we are the happier we will be, because holiness and happiness are inseparably bound together. It's only when we experience complete health that we will be able to relate in a loving and congenial manner to our families, friends, and others with whom we come in contact. Life will become a celebration of sharing! Service for Christ will become a way of life.

So, welcome to this study of "The Whole Woman—Fashioned in His Image." Get ready to grow to your full potential of wholeness. The best is yet to be!

2

Spiritual Health

"I am praying that all is well with you and that
your body is as healthy as I know your soul is."
(3 John 2, TLB)

It takes healthy trees to bear beautiful, luscious fruit!

The healthier the living organisms, the more lavishly they produce. But this production does not come automatically. The soil must first be properly cultivated and enriched. An exposure to sunlight and rain is an absolute necessity. Then—the miracle of fruit!

Spiritual Fruit

One of the most visible signs that a Christian woman is alive and well is that she is producing spiritual fruit that is both attractive and useful. In Gal. 5:22-23 St. Paul gives a list of fruit that will appear in the lives of those who have been nourished and filled with the Holy Spirit.

Let's look at some of this beautiful and desirable fruit.

Love

Loving is costly! How deeply—how sacrificially do we love?

I asked Jesus, "How much do you love me?"
"This much," He answered,
and stretched out His arms on the cross
and died.

This kind of love that comes only through the Holy Spirit is godly, pure, and enduring. It is supernatural! We find it fully described in the love chapter of the Bible (1 Corinthians 13).

These impressive words that measure the depth of Christian love were written by Walter Rinden.

For me to love—
is to commit myself,
freely and without reservation.

18

I am sincerely interested
in your happiness and well-being.
Whatever your needs are,
I will try to fulfill them
and will bend in my values
depending on the importance
of your need.
If you are lonely and need me,
I will be there.
If in that loneliness you need to talk,
I will listen.
If you need to listen,
I will talk.
If you need the strength
of human touch,
I will touch you.
If you need to be held
I will hold you.

Joy

"The joy of the Lord is your strength."
(Neh. 8:10)

There's a radiance about someone who is so joyful that it can't be hidden. You can't smother it; you can't keep it down! It's because *joy is a cousin to laughter.* Christian joy on the inside spills over in happiness on the outside.

Some people are like sugar bowls—they keep their sweetness on the inside. But not so with the radiance of joy. Cheerfulness becomes a therapeutic factor in your daily living. It even contributes tremendously to good health. It will—

aid in helping us digest our food,
relax us for a peaceful sleep,
help lift the weight of our burdens,
give us courage to face adversities.

Life becomes what we make it! Frown at the world and it frowns back at us—but laugh at the world and it will catch the contagion of our joy and laugh with us. As Dr. Robert Schuller of the Crystal Cathedral so often says, "Knock out the gloom and doom from your life." Jesus promised that His joy would be in us and our joy would be complete (John 15:11).

So let's make a reputation for ourselves by being happy, radiant, cheerful, glad! Demonstrate to the world a godly joy!

Peace

> "He will keep in perfect peace
> all those who trust in him."
> (Isa. 26:3, TLB)

Peace is evidenced by a quiet heart. Our world would know peace if only men and women were at peace with themselves. It's so easy for some to blame others for their inner frustrations and turmoil and trouble when the battle is raging from within their own souls.

Just as contentment does not depend on where we are but what we are, so inner peace is mental rather than circumstantial. Outwardly, everything surrounding our lives may be in conflict—but inwardly, there can be peace as calm as a smooth-flowing river. For no storm of life has the power to take from us the peace we have in Christ. This peace that "will guard *[our]* hearts and [our] minds in Christ Jesus" (Phil. 4:7). And how rewarding it is to see this peace communicated to those who need peace of mind and heart.

Martha lay dying. She had been nudged by the Lord many months before about sharing her faith with Juanita, an unsaved friend.

Her schedule had been too full—or so she had thought. And she had never quite gotten around to following the prompting of the Holy Spirit. Now her time was swiftly passing. She asked her daughter to contact her friend. "Please ask her to come and see me, both for her own sake and mine."

When Juanita came, Martha could speak only a few words before she died. But evidently they were enough.

Her friend knelt beside the bed while still holding Martha's hand. She pledged to God that He could use her life to fill the vacancy left in His vineyard by Martha's passing.

One soul was at peace with God in heaven—another had found peace that passes all understanding!

There is no peace, no joy, no satisfaction like fulfilling God's mission for ourselves—at the time when He speaks. One hour, one day, one week—may be too late!

Patience

> "Be still before the Lord and
> wait patiently for him."
> (Ps. 37:7)

There's an interesting story told about the great New England preacher, Phillips Brooks. He was known for his poise and self-control. However, his more intimate friends had seen him on more than one occasion when he suffered moments of frustration and irritability.

One day Dr. Brooks was seen pacing the floor like a caged animal. "What is the trouble, Sir?" asked his friend. "You look greatly disturbed."

"The trouble is, I'm in a hurry and God isn't," responded the impatient Dr. Brooks.

Have you ever been there? Have you tried to turn the hands of the clock ahead in order to speed up God's timing—or back to give more hours in the day? We are so prone to forget that God's timing is never off—not even one second.

"Is there real love for God without patience?" asked John Wesley. "Humility and patience are the surest proofs of the increase of love."

"Be completely humble and gentle;
be patient, bearing with one another
in love."
(Eph. 4:2)

When we open ourselves up for the gift of God's patience we should be prepared to receive it packaged in any way He sees fit. "I prayed for patience and God gave me polio!" was the testimony of a young woman whom my husband and I pastored. The permanent limp with which she walked after her illness slowed her down so that she could keep in step with those who lagged behind.

Patience can calm the spirit so that we can demonstrate this virtue while under the most distressing situations or in times of extreme pressure.

Kindness

Kindness is something you can feel. It's a language the blind can see and the deaf can hear. Kindness involves many forms of behavior:

Being considerate
Understanding
Courteous
Thoughtful
Tender
Gracious

21

This behavior pattern can become a spiritual habit as we obey the impulses and nudges of the Holy Spirit.

The lack of courtesy and kindness shown in the home between husband and wife is the basic cause of many marriage failures today. When two people no longer make the effort to show little courtesies to each other, it's time to take inventory of their relationship. The fire is burning low—too low! The romance of a marriage must be nourished. Acts of kindness are the most visible way of saying, "I love you," "I respect you," "You are special to me!"

Children learn from observing. They usually act out what they see and mimic what they hear.

Our hurting world is reaching out for the tenderness and sweetness that kindness offers. So practice it today—don't delay! Do it in the name of Jesus and for His glory.

You cannot do a kindness too soon
because you will never know how soon it will be too late.

Goodness

When we are born into the family of God His goodness is imparted to us. But just as fruit must grow and develop, so must the Christian's goodness.

You are writing a gospel,
A chapter each day,
By deeds that you do,
By words that you say.
Men read what you write,
Whether faithless or true,
Say, what is the gospel
According to you?[1]

Our good deeds will emulate Christ in a practical way. You remember the Bible story of Dorcas in Acts 9:36. It's an effective example of the "fruit of goodness," as she modeled generosity from a kind and gentle heart to her corner of the world.

Faithfulness

Someone has called the 11th chapter of Hebrews "God's Hall of Fame." It gives mini-biographies of men and women who demonstrated faithfulness by being full-of-faith.

Those who receive the gift of faith are still being inducted into this hall of fame.

A devoted missionary served for 15 years without the encouragement of one convert. Yet, he remained faithful. He continued to love, to share, to invite people to Christ.

Then an epidemic came. The natives fled like scared rabbits, abandoning the critically sick. Faithfully the missionary labored day and night in an attempt to save as many lives as possible. Finally, he too succumbed to the dreaded disease and joined the list of casualties. Had he given his life in vain? No! Another missionary was assigned to replace him, and many turned to Christ. Why? Because of the beloved missionary who gave his life for them.

His actions had proven to them that, "Greater love has no one than this, that one lay down his life for his friends." His faithfulness in time of need did what words could not do.

Many of us will not make headlines with spectacular feats of faith during our lifetime. But the gift of faithfulness will guarantee the greatest reward of all.

"Be faithful, even to the point of death,
and I will give you the crown of life."
(Rev. 2:10)

Gentleness and Self-control

These last Spirit-gifts are really two sides of the same spiritual coin. Gentleness is a quality of spirit that is demonstrated in self-control. Sanctification *cleanses* self, it does not *destroy* it. Self-will is crucified with Christ, but the new, Spirit-filled self is very much alive.

"You have taken off your old self with its practices
and have put on the new self, which is being renewed
in knowledge in the image of its Creator."
(Col. 3:9-10)

Listen to this beautiful testimony of one of my favorite Christian leaders and writers, Dr. E. Stanley Jones.

I laid at His feet a self of which I was ashamed, couldn't control, and couldn't live with; and to my glad astonishment He took that self, remade it, consecrated it to Kingdom purposes, gave it back to me, a self I can now live with gladly and joyously and comfortably.[2]

"Exhibit A" of self-control is the gentle Jesus. Even when He drove the corrupt moneychangers out of the Temple He was not out of control. He did not lose His temper. He held it! This display of righteous anger showed the kind of temper that gives a steel hammer its strength. This is what Eph. 4:26 means: "In your anger do not sin."

23

When we are Spirit-controlled, we are self-controlled. Yielded to His mastery, God takes charge. Only then can we demonstrate the gentleness of spirit that lets others know that "for . . . me, to live is Christ" (Phil. 1:21).

Going Toward Our Goals

The world has been made more beautiful by the dreamers of our day—the composer, the poet, the painter, the inventor, the sculptor. By cherishing their visions, their lofty ideals, they became masters of their own attainable dreams. In much the same way spiritual achievements are the consummation of holy aspiration. We will become as small as our lowest desire or as great as our highest dream. We will be limited only by the goals we set. Then the strength of our efforts will be the measure of our results. *We will seldom produce in quality and quantity more than we can envision within our own minds.*

It's possible that His will may take us through the deep waters of adversities. Some charismatic "health and wealth" preachers on television tell us that it is always God's will to deliver us from all physical and mental suffering. It is certainly true that Jesus performed miracles of divine healing—and still does. I have been the recipient of His divine touch more than once. But if it is within the will of God that everyone be healed, why was St. Paul not healed when he prayed for release from his "thorn in the flesh"? Why do some devout Christians suffer today?

The only logical answer is that divine healing is one realm of God's power and grace where He reserves the sovereign right to choose whether He will extend His touch or withhold it. Romans 8:28 assures us that "in *all things* God works for the good of those who love him" (italics added).

> *To be deprived of health may be hard to bear*
> *And harder perhaps to understand.*
> *Yet, we cannot measure Divine Providence*
> *By the yardstick of human mentality.*
> *What we think of as evil may well be*
> *The instruments with which He fashions*
> *Us for better things to come.*
>
> Author unknown

Someone has commented that when we enter heaven we will not be checked over for medals but for scars. So, if and when suffering comes to us, let's not fight it or try to evade it. Try thanking Jesus for the opportunity to prove our true discipleship by identifying with His suffering for us.

Perseverance

No one can possibly succeed by quitting—or win by giving up prematurely.

> A high school coach who was noted for producing a winning track team, enforced only one basic rule. Every participant entering the race must eventually cross the finish line—no matter what!
>
> If they became exhausted, they could stop and take a few minutes to get their breath, but they were never to get off the track. They might have excruciating cramps in their legs—that meant that they were to let up and give their muscles a chance to relax. But they were to stay on the track until they ultimately crossed the finish line.
>
> For the participant who came in first, his reward would speak for itself. He had been faithful in applying himself through strict discipline, persistence, and hard work. By so doing he had developed a strong athletic body and had also conditioned his mind for speed and endurance. Those who finished in fourth, eighth, or twelfth place but had diligently done their best could also consider themselves winners.
>
> Holding out to the end was the essence of victory!

This Christian coach, without quoting scripture, was teaching his students Heb. 12:1-2. "Let us throw off everything that hinders and . . . entangles, and let us run with perseverance the race marked out for us."

God's promises bring strength when we are tempted to drop out of life's race. Here is a great source of encouragement—"your strength will equal your days" (Deut. 33:25). This will enable us to triumph over any adversity.

Our Ultimate Goal

However, God has given to each one of us the power of choice. *Where we place our priorities on the scale of spiritual values will be the most crucial choice of life.* On this decision will hang our success or failure, improvement or degeneration. *In the final sense, our eter-*

nal destiny will be determined by our priorities. Proper choices in life will automatically lead to divine dividends.

Are you disappointed with your life's accomplishments? Have you looked in vain for some remarkable touch of genius in your life or for some brilliant gift of distinction? As of this day you may feel from your vantage point that everything about you remains ordinary, insignificant, and dull. You hear people speak of allowing God to work miracles through their lives. You are asking, "What's wrong with me? Why does God continually pass me by? I would like to be recognized for something! To be someone special!" If these are your sentiments today, then listen to Luke 14:23, where we are reminded that *God calls many of His most valued workers from the unknown multitudes.* By performing the most common, menial tasks, you may be doing far better than you know.

Your success in becoming a whole person in spirit, soul, and body will identify you as an extraordinary Christian—fashioned in His image and fruitful in His service. The human eye obviously sees only the present. God sees the end results. Remember, we are running for the duration, for the finish line. All things in between are merely teaching experiences. By God's help we will be able to testify, "I have fought the good fight, . . . I have kept the faith" (2 Tim. 4:7). This must be *our ultimate goal* and destiny—a goal that's attainable and a destiny that's eternal!

Let Us Pray

"Don't worry about anything; instead, pray about everything; tell God your needs and don't forget to thank him for his answers. If you do this you will experience God's peace, which is far more wonderful than the human mind can understand. His peace will keep your thoughts and your hearts quiet and at rest as you trust in Christ Jesus" (Phil. 4:6-7, TLB).

A solitary time each day in quiet communion with Christ is an absolute must! We cannot allow it to become an optional tryst that we casually omit or observe at will. If Jesus rarely hears from us, it means that our priorities need to be reshuffled. It's no wonder that there are times when God's presence seems dim and we feel "out of touch." Some walk through an entire day without once recognizing Him as Lord.

This story dramatically illustrates this truth.

The story is told of Victoria, the queen of England, who was caught in a heavy rainstorm one day during a walk among the woods at her summer residence in Balmoral. Spotting a small, rugged cottage nearby, the queen's feet took her swiftly over the rough grounds and tall grass. Waiting for a response to her frantic knock on the door of the cottage, she stood in the drenching rain with every part of her body getting thoroughly soaked. At long last an elderly woman opened the door, but only wide enough to see who was knocking.

Having little contact with the outside world, the woman did not recognize the queen. She stood looking at her with indifference and almost irritation.

The queen kindly asked if she might borrow an umbrella. After a scrutinizing look, the elder woman grudgingly handed the queen the older of two umbrellas that hung on a rack near the door. One was scarcely used, the other badly torn and dilapidated. The queen, recognizing that she had no choice, gratefully accepted the worn umbrella and was on her way.

Early the following morning a servant from the royal palace returned the battered umbrella in the name of Queen Victoria. Her note expressed only appreciation for the help that had been given to her.

The elderly woman was totally devastated. Imagine the embarrassment and the humiliation of this little woman when she realized the injustice she had paid the Queen of England.

"If only I had known!" She repeated over and over again. "I would have given her my best."

Certainly none of us would intentionally fail to give proper recognition to the King of Kings. However, could it be that we have been so busy looking at other faces that His countenance has been forgotten? If we neglect to commune consciously with Him on a regular basis, are we not giving Him less than our best?

General Lord Astley, before going into the battle of Edgehill in 1642, prayed a short but very significant prayer.

O Lord, you know how busy we will be today. If we by chance forget you, please do not forget us. For Christ's sake. Amen.

A short prayer like that is better than no prayer at all, but how far superior was Martin Luther's example. He felt that the busier he was the more time he should allocate to renewing the source of his strength and faith through prayer. He knew that he could not stand in the face of adversity or retain a godly spirit of love without the daily supply of courage and hope that came from his time spent with the Lord.

Our Quiet Time

The biographer of Samuel Chadwick wrote:

> He was essentially a man of prayer. Every morning he would be astir shortly after six o'clock, and he kept a little room which was his private sanctum for his quiet hour before breakfast. He was mighty in public prayer because he was constant in private devotion. . . . When he prayed he expected God to do something. "I wish I had prayed more," he wrote toward the end of his life, "even if I had worked less; and from the bottom of my heart, I wish I had prayed better."[3]

Do we make it a point to find a place of solitude in order to be alone with God? Here is the story of a British soldier who did.

> One night as he was creeping stealthily back to his quarters from a nearby clump of trees, he heard a voice calling out to him. "Who's there?" shouted a sentry. "What are you doing out here?"
>
> The soldier's explanation did not satisfy the guard. "Come with me," he said with a sneer. "You will tell this story to the commanding officer!"
>
> The soldier quietly explained to the commander, "I went into the woods so I could be alone to pray. This is my only defense."
>
> The officer asked if he had been in the habit of spending a lot of time in private prayer. "Yes, Sir," answered the soldier.
>
> "Then, down on your knees and pray now!" demanded the officer. The soldier knelt and began to pray earnestly and without hesitancy.
>
> When he had finished his prayer the officer said, "I believe your story. If you hadn't often prayed alone, you couldn't have done so well here! You are dismissed."[4]

The quality of our lives will always reflect the beauty of Christ when we spend time in communion with Him.

Faith and Miracle

Christ takes us beyond the level of hope to the prayer of faith. Only then do we move to a plane of expectation. It's impossible for prayer to work unless we have faith. The Lord encourages us with the promise, you can have anything you ask in prayer—if you believe (Matt. 21:22). Nothing will contribute more to faith-"full" lives than seeing mountains moved in answer to believing prayer.

Real prayer is costly! It is a vital, daily renewing experience of fellowship with God that is unselfish. We must be prepared for Him to reveal what we really are. If there are feelings of pride, self-indulgence, superiority, or unkindness, they must go! In their place will be a growing and maturing in the deeper things of Christ—peace, joy, contentment, compassion, faith.

True faith not only helps us compose an effective prayer to Christ, but it also aids us in trusting Him enough to commit it to His care. Then, and only then, can we receive from God that for which we ask. God does not force from our grasp anything or anybody. We must let go voluntarily. This demonstrates an unconditional faith in Him.

There are times when God does the extraordinary in response to faith. He not only heals the sin-sick soul but the body as well. My youngest sister is a living example of such a miracle.

> Terri, desperately ill, had undergone major surgery. It was followed by an unbelievable number of complications. The physicians and nurses on her case all despaired of her life. She hung, literally, between life and death for weeks.

> Several hundred people joined the members of our family in prayer for her recovery. We could only believe and trust that the Lord would choose to prove His power by an act of divine healing. The members of our family kept a vigil day and night.

> One Wednesday night I felt impressed to go to the Porterville Church of the Nazarene where I asked Pastor Wil Spaite to anoint me on behalf of Terri. Many members in the congregation had known Terri since she was a young girl. They really cared about her, and the earnestness of their prayers that night lifted my spirit.

> Later that evening in a phone conversation with my husband, I told him that for the first time my faith was strengthened to the point where I could believe that Terri was going to make it!

> Another special boost to my faith came a few days later when I took General Superintendent George Coulter, together with Pastor Spaite, into the intensive care ward where Terri lay critically ill. As these elders laid their hands on her and prayed the prayer of faith for her divine healing, I felt the presence of God in that room.

> We will never know whose prayer really touched the heart of God for my sister—or if it was our combined faith that moved the hand of God. It really doesn't matter! We just give praise to Him today that our lovely sister is well—and with a grateful heart is obediently serving Christ. She is a walking miracle of divine grace.

Faith has been described in mathematical terms like this:

> It subtracts weaknesses;
>> It adds power;
>>> It divides difficulties;
>>>> It multiplies possibilities.

Faith drops its letter in the mailbox and lets it go. Distrust holds onto the edge of it and wonders why the answer never comes. May we exercise such "prayer faith" that God will entrust to us the joy and privilege of representing Jesus in praying for others.

Prayer and Prodigals

We may not always be certain that we are praying within the divine will. But since Christ died for lost souls, of this one petition we can be sure. Though ultimately the sinner must make the choice to accept Christ's offer of salvation, our faith coupled with God's convicting power can make it more difficult for a sinful soul to reject Him. Let us be sensitive to the lost and obedient to God's promptings to lift them up in prayer.

A great prayer concern for many parents today is how to reach their wayward children for Christ.

A mother had prayed many years for her younger son, Gary, but he continued to reject the Lord of her life. Now he was to leave in two days for a distant city to work.

Her mother instinct told her that she should make one last attempt to bring her son to Christ. "Son, would you do your mother a special favor before you leave town? At the Art Center there is an unusually beautiful painting that I'd like you to see." Having no idea why, he consented to go.

On arriving at the Art Center, the hostess directed him to the number of the display room that his mother had given him. He opened the door, but finding a man kneeling at the front of the room, he softly closed it. After a few moments he again opened and closed it in respect to the man still in prayer. After several minutes had passed and the man still remained on his knees, Gary quietly walked to the front of the room. Only then did he realize that the kneeling man was part of the picture. It was the scene of Christ in Gethsemane.

With a sober countenance he stood looking intently at the face of Jesus. He was visibly moved by what he saw. Then he left the room and walked back home. Without waiting for any questions from his mother, he asked if she would return to the Art Center with him on the next day.

As he and his mother stood before the great painting together, he said, "Mother, you always told me that Jesus gave His life voluntarily for us—that He did it because He loved so much. Then why the sad, disturbed countenance?"

"Son, I'm not sure," said his mother. "Perhaps it's because His time had come to leave this world and there were still so many needs unmet down here. And He may have been concerned about the disciples carrying out His mission here on earth. For

30

even then the three disciples who had been asked to stay awake and pray were fast asleep."

Suddenly Gary dropped to his knees in front of the picture and for several minutes gazed into the face of Christ. Then he stood, straightened his shoulders, and said, "Oh, Man of God, if there is anything You have left undone that I can do, I am Yours to command."

God's timing is not always our timing, nor His ways our ways. This is why absolute trust in Christ must be exercised. This mother will always believe that God gave her the one plan that would bring her wayward son to his knees in humility and repentance before Jesus.

Keep Praying

Let's look at four steps that I believe are imperative if we are to keep the channels of communication open, giving God a free rein to work. Yes, free to work some miracles of grace through the prayers of each one of us. Remember, we seek only those answers to prayer that will glorify Christ.

1. **Commitment** means that not a square inch of our heart is closed off to Christ. We are totally His! This includes our will. With Christ we say, "Father, . . . not my will, but yours be done" (Luke 22:42). Total commitment means that we now imitate Christ. We act like Him, talk like Him, love like He loved and, if necessary, share His suffering.

Everything we are and everything that we have belongs to the Master. He controls us—body, mind, and soul!

2. **Trust** is when we accept, without question, God's Word to be true and uncompromising. Where there is perfect love, there is trust! Jesus so trusted His Heavenly Father that He never rehearsed present circumstances. Can we trust Him in like manner so that trials, conflicts, testings, and sorrow are accepted as a part of God's divine plan of discipline rather than as misfortunes?

The Book of James teaches us to put to the test what we claim to believe by doing it! Have we reached the level of achieving faith?

Trust and faith means that we walk obediently and submissively to His will—no matter what!

3. **Communion** is nothing less than the totality of the soul conversing with God the Father. When we pray with a pure heart we have every right to insert a personal pronoun, making every promise

of God our very own. We're not just a number: our name is recorded in the Royal Family Album. And as a Father, God waits to give us all the attention we need. We have only to ask.

Jesus told His disciples a parable to show them that they should *always pray and not give up! Have we prayed long enough?* We all have a desire for the instantaneous—instant pudding, coffee, tea, and even prayer answers. We cannot always know God's timetable. So *let's keep praying—the answer may be on its way within the hour!*

4. **Praise** is all too often the forgotten step in experiencing a miracle through prayer. It can have an explosive quality! It has transforming power!

"True praise is a worthy sacrifice;
this really honors me."
(Ps. 50:23, TLB)

Let me repeat what I said under trust. Jesus never rehearsed present circumstances. He spoke the desired results. What is faith? The evidence of things not yet seen or felt. So what do we do? We praise God for the desired results of our prayers.

Therapy of Praise

Psalm 34:1 admonishes us to bless the Lord at all times and let His praise always be on our lips. It didn't say if and when the sun is shining and every circumstance is of our choosing. No, because often the only option we have is the attitude we demonstrate in a given situation. We learn to praise the Lord at all times when our faith has been lifted to the level that doesn't demand the answer to all the "whys" of life.

Yes, praise comes from hearts that totally accept God's plan—His will. We don't take a bargaining position. We don't call the moves. We don't try to manipulate God.

We must arrive at the place one person did when he wrote on a placard, "Praise the Lord anyhow." Then we can accept the fact that there is beauty to be experienced in every situation. We have but to trust God to help us find it. This can be the master key to overcoming anything with praise and thanksgiving. It doesn't mean that there aren't "crying days" when grief is deep and crushing. We're only human and God gave us emotions as a means of release. No one is penalized for shedding an emotional tear. But in the midst of our anguish we can still feel praise in our hearts toward Him and thankfulness for His hand at work in our lives.

How can we praise God when the rug has been pulled from beneath our feet? When the one person whom we loved more than life itself has been taken from us? Here is the testimony of one who experienced such a loss.

Death had recently taken the loving companion from a dear and cherished friend. In her grief and pain she felt that every light had suddenly gone out of her life.

Her faith had received a terrible jolt! She had believed for a miracle of divine healing. Her husband in the prime of his life was not prepared to let go of the many goals and aspirations not yet accomplished for the Lord.

Although my friend knew that God never makes a mistake, she was finding it extremely difficult to see beyond this life—beyond death. She could only feel the depth of her sorrowing heart.

But one morning as she was praying the Lord seemed to say, you have grieved long enough! It's time for you to go on with your life. I have work for you to do for Me!

Don't you realize the many things for which you have to be grateful? Your family, financial security, a host of friends, and good health? All of these are blessings from Me. Isn't it enough to give you a joyful heart?

Suddenly it was like God had lifted a veil from before her eyes. For the first time since her husband's death she could see things in their proper perspective. She knew she was loved. She knew God still cared for her.

Never again was she to be bothered by the lack of a grateful heart and the inability to praise God—even through adversity and disappointments. Yes, and even through sorrow!

My friend was still lonely for her husband. Her sorrow had not diminished. But the strength of the Lord was made strong in her weakness; His grace acted as a soothing oil for her aching heart; His divine love helped fill the human vacuum left by her husband's passing. God never takes away without giving something in return. Why? Because He is a just God! A loving God!

If faith is the hinge that opens the door to opportunity, it is fortitude that gives us the strength to walk through that door. Who would know better than Helen Keller? She wrote, *"Dark as my path may seem to others, I carry a magic light in my heart."* And this heavenly light is what will give us a song in the night and a note of praise on our lips.

3

Spiritual Growth

Through divine power, we are nourished with every essential ingredient for growth, maturity, and productivity. This inner nourishment will produce a person who is "whole" and "balanced."

Scriptural Nourishment

Any born-again individual will soon become anemic spiritually without the daily nourishment of the Holy Scriptures. They become our guidebook to eternal life. The Bible, God's inspired Word, is the world's most remarkable book—because of its timelessness, its universality, its survival, but most of all for its impact and influence on human life. To personally know Christ is to internalize His Word!

We can accomplish many things through mere human endeavor. Our moods can be lifted and changed; our minds enlightened and refreshed; our muscles strengthened and exercised. But studying the Word of God gives us so much more. It gives us a source of re-creation that goes far deeper than any human effort can offer.

This valued book is our greatest source of "faith development" in Christ. It talks to us like a good friend. It becomes a powerful, shaping force in our lives. Through faith attained by studying the Word, we can slay *two great enemies of spiritual life—doubt and fear.* It also gives us a sense of authority in communicating His truth.

"Consequently, faith comes from hearing
the message, and the message is heard
through the word of Christ."
(Rom. 10:17)

Wisdom is received through faithful attention to the teaching of the Word. As we study His Word, we will be taught, rebuked, corrected, and trained in righteousness so that as women of Christ we may be equipped for the Christian service He has for us to render.

Study Methods

The question is frequently asked concerning the best method for studying the Word of God. One principle should always be observed. Don't neglect certain books of the Bible that seem to be less inspiring and helpful than others. "All scripture is given by inspiration of God, and is profitable" (2 Tim. 3:16, KJV). Read a portion in the Old and New Testament in each devotional period if possible.

Personally, I'm never quite satisfied in my own heart unless my reading gives me something uplifting, challenging, and/or strengthening for that particular day. Sometimes I fail to find this by reading only in the Old Testament.

A Marked Bible

One Bible scholar says he reads from a *new* Bible every year. He enjoys underlining new truth as God speaks to him. In going back through his Bibles he has been amazed how differently the Bibles are marked. This, of course, is how God works in our lives. He is continually molding us through His truth.

Have you tried using colored pens or pencils for marking different promises of God as you study the Bible? It makes easy reading when you have a particular need immediately! Some days I enjoy opening my Bible and reading only those portions that are underlined. *A marked Bible is a treasured Bible!* You can decide on your own color scheme, but these colors were the ones recommended to me:

> . . . black for sin
> . . . red for redemption and salvation
> . . . blue for encouragement and comfort
> . . . green for faith
> . . . yellow for holiness
> . . . purple for Christ's coming

Other Helps

Many of us also find daily devotional guides to be very helpful. They provide valuable insights into the meaning of selected scriptures and also contribute inspirational comment on these passages. One of my favorites is Mrs. Charles Cowman's *Streams in the Desert.* I have used it for many years with great personal benefit. Another classic is Oswald Chambers' *My Utmost for His Highest.*

One of the fine contemporary guides is *Come Ye Apart,* which is a devotional quarterly following the Sunday School lessons.

Many excellent commentaries on the Bible are available. Two of these are Adam Clarke's and the *Beacon Bible Commentary. Beacon Bible Expositions* is a set of devotional commentaries on the New Testament, especially designed for laypersons, and another good investment. Sets of commentaries can be purchased one volume at a time and make nice gifts. These provide helpful interpretations of hard-to-understand passages. It would be well to consult one of these when the meaning of a scripture is unclear.

Anyone who knew Missionary Harmon Schmelzenbach recognized that the Word of God was the greatest creative force in his life. He read it, spoke it, lived it, shared it. Rev. Schmelzenbach learned from personal experience that—

You only pray well when you can pray God's Word.

You only live well when you follow His pattern.

You only speak well when He speaks through you.

You only love well when His love flows through your life.

This poem was taken from the flyleaf of Rev. Schmelzenbach's Bible:

> *Lay any burden upon me,*
> *Only sustain me;*
> *Send me anywhere,*
> *Only go with me;*
> *Sever any tie*
> *But that one which*
> *Binds me to Thy service*
> *And to Thy heart*

If ever there was a man of God committed to His mission, it was Harmon Schmelzenbach. This, no doubt, came about largely because he knew the Word of God so well. And to know the Word of God was to obey its truth.

Being well versed in the Holy Scriptures will give us confidence in communicating His Word. It will add enthusiasm to our lives and make us dynamic in our service.

20/20 Spiritual Vision

The eye is one of the most precious and useful physical organs. Careful attention is given to preserving sight through maintaining healthy eyes. No consideration of "spiritual health" would be complete without observing the condition of our spiritual vision.

What a contrast when God lifts our sight from the sinful to the sanctified. Before salvation we saw only the materialistic and self-gratifying things of this life. Now it's like a veil has been lifted and we have a clear view of God and eternity. This shuts out the sight of many temporal, worldly things. Mary James wrote:

> *Since my eyes were fixed on Jesus,*
> *I've lost sight of all beside,*
> *So enchained my spirit's vision,*
> *Looking at the Crucified.*[5]

One of the absolute evidences of new spiritual sight is the way we see people. Color and race, educational and economic status suddenly become secondary. Our primary focus is now upon their spiritual well-being. We see them through Jesus' eyes.

A young woman sat waiting her turn to be interviewed by a missionary board. This meeting was a routine procedure for those planning to return to the mission field. Her furlough was over. She was ready to return to the people she loved. She had been cautious not to become too comfortable in the luxuries of her own country. Her thoughts and concerns were still with her adopted homeland of India.

Suddenly her reminiscing was cut short! Her name was being called. The board was ready to see her. Their first question was deliberately pointed. "Why do you want to return to India with its poverty and filth?"

Her countenance took on a sudden earnestness as she said, "Because I cannot sleep at night! When I close my eyes I see the pain-filled eyes of those dark-skinned people of India. Satan has used every trick to try and blur my vision. But my spiritual eyes look into eternity, and I can't get away from my God-given mission. I must open the eyes of these people that they might see Jesus; that they might know the pain that He suffered for them; that they are precious in His sight. I want those in India to know Jesus as I know Him."

This 20/20 spiritual vision is not a special gift for missionaries. *Every Christian everywhere has a responsibility to see the hurts and heartaches of mankind.* Especially must we be concerned about those whose sins have separated them from the love of God. We must be "haunted" by their hopelessness. This vision will bring compassion and awareness more clearly before us. And will, in turn, motivate us to bring the "Good News" of salvation to them.

Watching Our Words

What area of our lives is more essential to spiritual health than our daily speech? "If any man [woman] offend not in word, the same is a perfect man, and able also to bridle the whole body" (James 3:2, KJV). The Word of God emphasizes repeatedly the unlimited power of the spoken word.

> "Pleasant words are as an honeycomb,
> sweet to the soul, and health to the bones."
> (Prov. 16:24, KJV)

> "Death and life are in the power of the tongue."
> (Prov. 18:21, KJV)

> "He sent his word, and healed them."
> (Ps. 107:20, KJV)

> "The tongue that brings healing is a tree
> of life."
> (Prov. 15:4)

Jesus was the perfect example of making words work for Him. He spoke the world into existence; He raised His voice toward heaven and the multitude was fed; Jesus spoke and the storm was stilled; the Centurion said to Jesus, "Speak the word only and my servant shall be healed." He raised the dead and strengthened the weak—both by the word of His mouth.

If we are to master our tongues, Christ must first master our hearts. For, "Out of the abundance of the heart the mouth speaketh" (Matt. 12:34, KJV).

Dr. J. B. Chapman made reference to a young man who stood in the presence of Socrates. After a few moments of silence Socrates said, "Speak, lad, that I may see you." The words that proceed out of our mouths do allow others to see into our hearts. According to the Bible *the great test of a person's character is how he uses his tongue.* There is a time to speak and a time to be silent. Only God has the wisdom of placing within our mouths His words. Perhaps it would help if we would all pray this simple prayer at the beginning of each new day. *Lord, help my words to be tender and sweet today, for to-morrow I may have to eat them!*

Many situations will be worked out quietly and smoothly if we talk only with the Lord about them. Learn to confide in Him rather than even in your best friend. God who hears in secret, will never talk, will never break your confidence. What great lessons we can learn from the One who is altogether lovely! He will teach us that there is no better exercise for strengthening the heart—spiritually or physically—than reaching down and lifting people up. Who knows what fallen angel we may, even today, save from a state of despair by our kindly words of encouragement and hope.

Remember, *our words and speech are an accurate index of our moral and spiritual health.* Our character becomes the sum total of all our thoughts, and from our thoughts comes our speech. If our words are untrue and unkind, our souls are sickly and diseased. Negative thoughts are controlling us and will eventually defeat us. If the character of our speech has all the symptoms of health, they are just the opposite. Our words will be healing.

The Discipline of the Tongue

God's standard for the use of the tongue is pondered speech. Thoughtful words season rather than destroy. This is why *a perverse tongue is never compatible with a sanctified heart.*

> By your words, you shall be justified
> —but by your words you shall also be condemned.

Every word spoken from your lips and mine is doing one of two things: building up or tearing down; healing or destroying. Is it any surprise that the tongue is known as the most powerful tool we own?

There are few influences more wholesome than a good name. God's great controversy with Israel was because they had profaned His holy name by their unholy work (Ezekiel 36). There is nothing more grievous than when a reputation is needlessly and thoughtlessly damaged by a careless and malicious tongue. *The only muscle one needs to break down another's dignity or to destroy a life is the muscle in the mouth.* A conscientious woman stood to her feet in a women's Bible seminar. She was a new Christian. Something pertaining to Christians and their speech greatly disturbed her. Her question caused each one there to take a quick inventory of her own speech. "When someone insists on pouring garbage into your ears, what do you say?"

"I suppose she asked you not to tell anyone else," the chairman said. "Yes, in fact she did," the woman replied. "Then ask her why she's cluttering your mind with it." A good answer! Use it. It could rid you of trash bearers. Unless the news is good, don't pass it on— and don't listen. It will contaminate your thinking and your spirit. It may also cause you to be prejudiced.

One woman's suicide note read:
"They said . . ."
Something *they* said caused her to take her life.

Some people could easily miss eternal life unless and until they make restitutions concerning an unhealthy use of their tongue. If saying, "I'm sorry" is needed, then be obedient! It will be well worth the peace you gain in your heart.

Discipline will play a major role in honoring and pleasing God with our tongues. You might begin by praying this prayer with the Psalmist, "Let the words of my mouth . . . be acceptable in thy sight, O Lord" (Ps. 19:14, KJV). Then help answer that prayer by weighing your words carefully. This is a new day. How about making a fresh start? Just as there has to be an ounce of self-discipline to every ounce of talent, so it is in the discipline of the tongue.

This poem, written by an evangelist and good friend, is one that will help everyone in the "tongue business." Read it! Reflect on it! Then, pray it into being.

Little Foxes Spoil the Vines

It is the little words we've spoken,
Words we've spoken carelessly,
That fly like sharp betrayal arrows
And make a Gethsemane.
It is the little notes unwritten
To a dear friend in deep loss
That hang dead regrets around our neck
Like a heavy albatross.
So I pray to be a guardian
Over all I say and do . . .
Remembering what I sow, I reap,
And that life will soon be through.
So I will think before I speak
And put a censor on my tongue . . .
And apologize when I have killed
A song before it's sung.

—Charles Hastings Smith
Used by permission

Emerson wrote that *every opinion expressed by an individual makes a lasting impression, consciously or unconsciously, on the hearers.* A good exercise for spiritual health involving the tongue was given by a wise and godly woman to a group of young Christians:

If you hear anything nice about a person, be sure to pass on the information. If you have heard anything unkind, wrap it up and take it home with you. It will make good praying material as you enter your *secret* closet of prayer with the Father.

There is a special power of chain reaction in speaking words that are *Spirit-filled.* It's an active force that produces a healthy climate—starting from within oneself and inspiring those around us.

What happens when we have pure motives and our words are misunderstood, misinterpreted, even misquoted? Will you read the words of instruction on the tongue written by David in Psalm 140? Then commit your situation to the Lord. Our defense is *His business, His specialty!* Often, trying to defend ourselves when our actions and motives are pure only aggravates the situation. Even Satan himself cannot stain a pure character—he *may* damage our reputation! But if we are innocent, God will some day right all wrongs, and this places the responsibility on Him. It helps me to remember that no one was ever more misquoted or misunderstood than Jesus himself. Yet, He did only good. He never retaliated. He never stooped to the level of His accusers. His last words were a benediction.

> *'Twas a thief said the last*
> *kind word to Christ:*
> *Christ took the kindness*
> *and forgave the thief.*

The Ministry of Listening

Peter Marshall realized one day that he was constantly sending "night letters" to the Lord. Why? Because they didn't necessitate a two-way conversation. Was he concerned that the Lord might differ with him: might possibly have something to say that would not coincide with his plans and timetable?

Mr. Marshall knew that *failing to listen to God could mean a gradual deterioration of his own spiritual growth and maturity.* It could even be *spiritual suicide!* He prayed, as we must all pray, that God would slow him down from his schedule of feverish activities to a steady, unhurried pace so beautifully demonstrated by his Master. Then he could listen to God, even as Jesus did to His Father.

We must have the daily guidance of God's divine touch if we are to keep in step with Him. And *there's no way we can hear unless we are quiet long enough to listen.*

If anyone ever had reason to turn off His "earphones," it would have been Jesus! But instead of being offended by our much coming, He is grieved when we fail to take advantage of His sympathetic and loving ears. And just as Jesus lends His ears to us, we must listen to others.

Learn by Listening

Listening usually follows a pattern. Those who are unable to listen to the needs of others probably don't bother to listen to Christ. Anyone who learns—listens! This is why God gave us two ears and only one mouth. Some have never recognized the significance of this. The fact that listening can be twice as blessed as speaking is quite a revelation to some people!

Have you ever noticed that some women rarely stop talking long enough for their own questions to be answered? Some answer for you so they won't lose the platform for even one minute. When they do listen, it's only with a half ear of impatience, waiting for their chance to jump back in charge again.

Many people would probably never need to visit the office of a psychiatrist if Christians could learn the ministry of listening. These are the feelings expressed to me by one counselor. Most individuals could solve their own problems if they would only open up and talk. But to whom? So many ministers seem to feel obligated to talk rather than listen—I mean really listen—unhurriedly and attentively. The medical doctors don't or won't take the time; it's easier and faster to write a prescription. And what about us as Christian women? Do we really care enough to listen? Godly listening is not simply hearing words spoken but listening in love; entering into their sorrow; feeling their disappointments and bearing their burdens.

It is also important that we learn the art of listening to people without forming a judgment about their viewpoint before they have finished speaking. Do we make a real attempt to feel what they are saying? Are our ears and eyes sensitive to the unvoiced words in between the lines?

Praying to our friend, Jesus, is an unexcelled privilege, but there are times when some people need the ears and touch of human flesh. This is why solitary confinement in a prison is still considered the cruelest punishment of all. So let's do everything possible to keep the channels open for communication—whether it be with friends, family members, husband, wife, or children. *Once the door is closed, it's terribly hard to open again.*

Perhaps the reason why some who are in need of a listener find it so difficult to locate ears that are available is that too many of us "broadcast" too much and "receive" too little. These individuals needing help feel it's an imposition to unload their problems on those of us who seem to be barely creeping along under our own burdens. May God help us who have walked *in the way* longer than some to take our burdens to the Lord and leave them there. Then, be prepared to help lift the eyes of less mature Christians to the Solver of all problems, great or small.

Today the world needs women who have an open path to their hearts. If our eyes are open and our ears are sensitive, we can see the hurts and hear the agonizing sobs of women who say, "Nobody cares." Oh, what an opportunity for service some of us are missing!

A Telephone Triumph

In one of our pastorates we had one dear, devoted Christian woman who made it necessary to add an extension cord on our telephone. There was no one who had made herself more available to those in need than she. But there came a time in her life when she went through several months of utter depression, mentally and emotionally. It was as though Satan had her backed into a corner with a net tightly wrapped around her entire body. She was so mentally distressed that she had to release to someone those fears that seemed to threaten her day and night.

Often the phone would ring at the most inopportune time of the day for me—in the midst of cooking a meal, while preparing for guests, or when getting dressed for an appointment. After a few weeks of personal frustration, I called for the telephone company to add a 12-foot extension cord to the telephone in our family room. The phone could then be taken to the kitchen stove and sink, to our master bedroom and bath, and to our utility room or front door. My husband said to me one day, "Is there anything you have not done while you have been on the phone except correct the children?" I had to confess that *also* could be added to the list!

Here was a precious friend who needed not a voice to speak but a loving auditor with ears to hear. Many scriptures were quoted and prayers prayed over the telephone wires—but *after* she had talked! Sure, she had rehearsed her problems over and over again. But she needed to voice them again. So I listened! Often I would refer her to Bible verses, chapters, and even entire books to read that particular day—not once, but as often as it took to force Satan to flee from her. She needed desperately to lift her eyes to Christ and *His* victory; the victory He had for her if she would only believe!

If her phone call came at a time when it was impossible to listen, we set another time when her call would be returned. Never did I want her to feel that I did not care! Who knows how many times I listened to her, or to someone else, when possibly it was the most loving and constructive service I rendered for Christ all that day.

Just as suddenly as my friend dropped into the valley of depression she came out on the mountaintop. After victory was hers, she made a startling remark to me one day: *"If you had not been willing to listen to me during those dark days and nights, I'm sure I would have ended up in a mental hospital."*

There is a time to listen and a time to speak. Caution should be exercised in giving direct counsel or advice. Many times individuals already know the course of action they should take. These people should be encouraged to follow divine guidance and to use their own best judgment. If we provide solutions, this diminishes their ability to solve their own problems. Sooner or later they must learn to stand firmly on their own feet in decision-making. *There have been times when a counselor has given well-meaning but unwise advice that has resulted in irreparable damage.* For these and other reasons it's advisable to listen twice as much as we speak.

There are three things that no one can ever retrieve:
The spoken word.
The past life.
The neglected opportunity.

May we never neglect the opportunity that comes through the ministry of listening! Many souls otherwise lost could well spend eternity with Christ because of our sensitivity and obedience in this area.

Forgiveness—a Spiritual Release

Love is a creative force that can bring good out of evil. Jesus was the supreme proof of this fact when He brought redemption out of the Cross. "Father, forgive them, for they do not know what they are doing" (Luke 23:34).

Forgiving is a solo flight! No one else can share it with us or do it for us. Only Christ fully understands and has the power to help us. Many times I have heard people say, "I can love and I can forgive—but I can't forget." It's true that everything we hear or see or feel is recorded on our subconscious mind. But Jesus is able to take over our thoughts so that where there were hurts He will replace them with love and peace.

True forgiveness is when we bury the hatchet so deeply that the handle is under the ground too far to pull it up again—and again—and yet again. It means that *we tear up the IOUs.* Some people refuse to destroy the metal filing box just in case they choose to make that person suffer periodically.

Have people injured your reputation? If so, they are blighting their own character—destroying themselves. Pray for them! Even pity them if that helps—but forgive them!

Godly love, generously given, still melts the heart of hardened sinners. Right now—today—someone's soul may be hanging in the balance because there needs to be love and forgiveness expressed by one of us.

One day Canon Goldsmith, a much loved and devoted missionary, entrusted to his Indian servant a sum of money with which to buy supplies for the mission station. But instead of returning with the supplies the servant disappeared with the money.

Mr. Goldsmith was very distressed. For days he searched for his servant. Finally when he was found he went to him in deep humility and said, "I'm so sorry I paid you such small wages for your services that you had to stoop to something like thievery. If you will return to your job with me, I will raise your pay."

The servant was completely overwhelmed by this expression of love and confidence. He returned to the missionary's home and repented for betraying the faith that had been placed in him. He remained Goldsmith's devoted and trusted friend until his death.

How many of us might have marked him off as a thief and perhaps had difficulty in forgiving him. Mr. Goldsmith even went the second mile in humbling himself enough to ask the servant's forgiveness.

What happens when we encounter hurts, embarrassment, sometimes deliberately inflicted on us—when our rights have been violated? And when that individual never asks for forgiveness! Then we remember Jesus' example and follow His pattern. We aren't responsible for others and how they respond. God holds us accountable only for our own actions and attitudes. When we relinquish ourselves to Christ, we are His to command—so we forgive!

> Booker T. Washington, the noted Black American educator, once said, "I will never allow any man to drag me so low as to make me hate him."

It has been proven that harboring animosities can destroy. But forgiveness can heal and has actually been known to save a life. There is no medicine for dissipating the ills of the body that equals pure thoughts from a loving and forgiving spirit.

Henry Wadsworth Longfellow made a statement that should make it easier for anyone to forgive:

> If we could read the secret history of our enemies, we should find in each man's life sorrow and suffering enough to disarm all hostility.[6]

We Gain Through Pain

There are some truths that only sorrow can teach. When it comes, if we don't fight or reject it, some good can always come out of it. I have yet to see any great, truly influential Christian woman who has not gone through the valley of disappointment, tragedy, or sorrow.

> There was a young singer who had a beautiful voice and faultless technique. A great creative artist and musician was listening. He made this comment after the audition was over. "She has a good voice—but it isn't great. Not yet! But wait until something happens to break her heart and then she will sing with feeling. That will make her great!"

Although Satan can accomplish some things, even he realizes that only God is all-powerful. He knows that he is not only limited but also accountable to God. The Father has him on a leash, and when He says, "Satan, it is enough," he can go no farther. This knowledge helps me!

We are not to be fearful, distressed, deceived, nor intimidated. Rather, we're to be on our guard, calm and alert to Satan's devices. In times of uncertainty we wait! We do not speak. We do not act. Anytime there is a restraint in our spirit we do not go against it. We wait until God releases it. This is being sensitive to His Spirit. This is gaining ground through spiritual maturity.

The Whole Woman—Physically

4

Physical Wholeness

God has created our total personality to work as a whole, not as separate units. The soul and spirit, which are tabernacled in the body, are both involved in the health of an individual. They are to be kept in perfect alignment with each other.

Neglect the body and it becomes ill and useless.

Neglect the mind and it grows dull and stagnant.

Neglect the soul and it becomes insensitive to Christ.

The health and effectiveness of the outer person is always contingent on the health of the inner person. "A heart at peace gives life to the body" (Prov. 14:30). In Rom. 6:12-14 Paul warns us that one part cannot be neglected or touched by sin without the whole person being affected.

Therefore do not let sin reign in your mortal body so that you obey its evil desires. Do not offer the parts of your body to sin, as instruments of wickedness, but rather offer yourselves to God, as those who have been brought from death to life; and offer the parts of your body to him as instruments of righteousness. For sin shall not be your master, because you are not under law, but under grace.

By committing ourselves to Christ we can work together to enhance and build upon His original creation. It is the only way to be fashioned into the beautiful image of womanliness that will honor and please the Lord.

Why are some women born healthier and more attractive, physically, than others? Perhaps it's because God needed variety to accomplish the work of His kingdom—personalities who differ in color, size, skills, and even stamina. But knowing that we serve a just God, I believe He shows no favoritism in making the same provision available for each of us to enjoy the best health possible.

Inevitably *good health and good performance go together.* It's the only way we can function smoothly with the maximum effectiveness and the greatest longevity. But each part of the body is assigned a specific responsibility that it must assume.

Can you imagine what would happen if our inner, vital organs were removed? Our bodies would only be empty shells unable to function at all! The outer parts that do the performing—eyes, nose, legs, arms, mouth—would simply be like pieces of a mannequin. But when each part is supportive of the other, it strengthens the body as a whole. They work together harmoniously and effectively.

The Mind Bridles the Body

Let's look at what God's Word has to say about our personal responsibility for maintaining a healthy body:

> "Do you not know that in a race all the runners run, but only one gets the prize? Run in such a way as to get the prize. Everyone who competes in the games goes into strict training. They do it to get a crown that will not last; but we do it to get a crown that will last forever.
>
> "Therefore I do not run like a man [woman] running aimlessly; I do not fight like a man [person] beating the air. No, I beat my body and make it my slave so that after I have preached to others, I myself will not be disqualified for the prize" (1 Cor. 9:24-29).
>
> "Each of you should learn to control his [her] own body in a way that is holy and honorable" (1 Thess. 4:4).

In his book *Shade of His Hand* Oswald Chambers makes this interesting observation, "God made man (woman) a mixture of dust and Deity—[because] Jesus Christ manifested Himself in that dust, . . . [our] dust is . . . [our] glory, not . . . [our] shame."[7] The Psalmist declares:

> "For you created my inmost being;
> you knit me together in my mother's womb.
> I praise you because I am fearfully and
> wonderfully made" (Ps. 139:13-14).

This is why we must value our bodies enough to keep them in good functioning condition. In God's creative genius He made us in His image.

It's vital that we *think* health rather than illness; joy rather than pain; optimism rather than negativism. Since the body was created to obey the commands of the mind, you can actually build desires by the words that you speak. If you doubt it, try talking with yourself about what you should or should not do.

- you create a physical fitness program geared to your personal needs;
- you desire to retain, or regain, good health by body building, nutritious foods, and exercise;
- you verbally tell yourself that you refuse to do or eat anything that will undoubtedly do harm to the body that God created for His glory.

You have now set a physical law into motion that relates meaningfully to this biblical truth: "Now ye are the body of Christ, and members in particular" (1 Cor. 12:27, KJV).

If you continue to hold this pattern of thinking, your body will be obedient and conform. But if you change your trend of thought and start telling your body it's too tired for exercising; that your figure looks better than most; that others allow themselves the luxury of pampered eating (chocolates, potato chips, ice cream, pies, cakes) and why should you buckle under, then you are in trouble! Your body, dictated to by your will, is going to do what your mind says. In an instant you will have defeated your original intentions. We must program our thinking so that our words and spirit will merge into a harmonious demonstration of godly discipline.

There are times when we are unable to overcome some weaknesses in our physical bodies. But most of the time whether we live in sick or physically fit bodies will largely be the result of how we treat ourselves.

Remember, it's never too late to start a health program—*today would be a good time!* It's up to us to keep a tight grip on ourselves. No one else can do it for us. This is the privilege and responsibility of having a free will.

Health and Maturity

I heard Dr. Norman Vincent Peale remind a large group of his hearers that discipline is the price we pay for freedom of choice—that it's a liberator, physically and mentally. And if we are to keep fit for the Master's service, it will necessitate self-discipline as found in 1 Cor. 6:12-13. He impressed on our minds that it's impossible to glorify God in our bodies to the fullest extent if they are sickly, sluggish, and unmotivated. He asked that we examine our performance and achievements for Christ to see if the functioning of the physical body is hindering us from being at our best spiritually. Contrary to many people who feel that they have no control over their bodies, Dr. Peale says this is simply not true and gives as his reference 1 Cor.

9:24-27, "Everyone who competes in the games goes into strict training."

Yes, discipline is a mark of maturity. And good health eventually means good habits practiced through self-discipline. Without proper discipline and nurture—resulting in good habits—our bodies, as well as our character, will become powerless and defenseless.

God's purpose carried out in our lives will be determined largely by our choice of priorities. I have known some people who had a wonderful physical heritage but who destroyed their bodies by an unwillingness to pay the price of self-discipline.

So, what do we do? How do we respond? Do we tell ourselves that we are too busy to spare the time for the disciplining of the physical body? Perhaps tomorrow, next week, in a month things will right themselves; my schedule will slow down; I will not continue this mad race forever! Or do we take authority immediately—like right now, this very day! It wouldn't even hurt us to apologize to the Lord for our lack of sensitivity to our bodily needs.

Life is a precious gift, a God-given gift that we dare not take lightly. If your life and mine were worth the investment of His time and energy and creativity, then we have no option. We won't abuse it! We won't treat it like a useless garment to be thrown away because of a few visible flaws. We value it. We give it proper care. Yes, even a little tender loving care wouldn't be bad!

Even friends, well-meaning as they are, often are a contributing factor in upsetting perfectly good intentions on our part. You don't think so? Can anyone really influence you when self-discipline needs to be exercised?

Let me test you! How many times have you eaten heavy, fattening dessert, universally known to add nothing to good health, simply because you didn't want to offend your hostess? How often have you eaten a full meal when your stomach was pleading for only a cup of herbal tea, a piece of whole wheat toast, and perhaps a piece of fresh fruit? Do you ever eat late at night, then toss and turn all night trying to sleep on an overloaded stomach?

What we all need is to assert personal authority over our willpower. I believe our friends will understand and respect us for it; we will like ourselves better for it; and we will honor God by being good stewards of our bodies.

Is good health a luxury? Not if we value life! Not if the priorities of our lives are related to our entire future rather than just a one-day run. Let's pay the small price of being able to live at our full potential physically so we can live up to our full possibilities spiritually.

Health and Healing

How badly do we want health? Physicians remind us constantly that a periodic checkup is essential to retaining good health. If we are as intelligent as we should be, we will follow their suggestions. Faith in Christ is not hampered by using good common sense. Doctors are provided for our benefit when the Lord does not choose to make us a recipient of His direct healing touch.

God is our Great Physician and can heal anyone at any time within His divine will. In the Word we are reminded that the Lord our God in the midst of us is mighty. If we are willing to appropriate His mighty power and strength into our redeemed bodies, He will fill them with His own energizing, vitalizing personality.

Divine healing in any area of our lives is simply divine life. It says that Christ has dominion over the body, over our whole being.

There are no specialists in the field of medicine who have enough earned degrees to really cure anyone by themselves. Only God heals. Any surgeon who uses his skills in the preservation of life will readily acknowledge also that without the cooperation of a patient in helping the healing process, that patient will rarely become well. A physician removes the cause of a disease or repairs an injury. Then his role becomes that of a director. The rest is up to the patient.

A dramatic case that demonstrates the validity of this truth was given at a conference on "Mental Health and Attitudes."

Two young men had been college friends. George was highly intelligent and extremely motivated. He worked with sheer determination to bring to fruition his life's goals and dreams. And was succeeding!

His friend Peter was equally intelligent and possessed all the natural gifts for becoming a success. But unlike George, he lacked the inner motivation and persistence needed for achieving—professionally, spiritually, or physically.

In a state of frustration and disappointment, Peter took to hard drugs and liquor. One night while under the influence of drugs he went to George and asked him for money. Knowing why he wanted it, George had to refuse him.

In a rage Peter took a long knife and stabbed George repeatedly, unaware of the crime he was committing on his very best friend.

In a coma, George lingered for days between life and death. When he finally regained consciousness and was on his way to recovery, his physician made this statement. "George, I despaired of your life. If your mental attitude toward Peter had not been positive, your body would not have been free to heal itself and you would not be alive today. But you said repeatedly, 'Peter, I forgive you. It's all right. You didn't know what you were doing.' Because of this love you enjoyed peace of mind and heart. Consequently, all your energy was released to the task of healing the wounds inflicted on your body. If there had been an inner conflict, it would have been curtains for you!"

All healing comes from the Great Physician whether it be in the area of attitudes, a forgiving spirit, a physical ailment, or a sinful heart.

The Therapy of Work

Living a life that is truly "whole" necessitates a daily renewal of all our physical powers through labor, worship, recreation, and rest. God's Word paints a vivid picture when it says, "In the sweat of thy face shalt thou eat bread." This means that He did not intend that all labor would be lit up with joy and satisfaction. Millions work at jobs every day that are anything but creative and rewarding. They are monotonous, routine, and sheer drudgery. However, it is gratifying to know that all honest labor done in the will of God is an acceptable worship to Him. Dr. Charles Mayo, founder of the Mayo Clinic, said that he had never found anyone who had died because of good healthy labor.

There is no substitute for work, either physically or mentally. Think for a moment of the truly successful people, past or present, in any area of life. They have worked to succeed. Success does not just happen!

Some people who possessed few special talents and little natural ability have become experts in their particular field of endeavor. How? By learning the art and value of work. That is the secret of some uneducated millionaires today.

Anyone worthy of the name "Christian" cannot allow idleness to become a part of her personality. Laziness is an act of disobedience to God. It can ultimately paralyze one's life into *nothingness!*

We must exercise and socialize; rest and worship—but we must also work. If our talents and abilities are sparse, we work all the harder. And today the Holy Spirit is anxious to work through every aspect of every personality. If we love God, *really love Him,* then we work for Him! We give all we have. If we are privileged to live tomorrow, it will be treated as a bonus day. We will greet the day eagerly with joy and gratitude. It's another day to serve Christ; to love, to laugh, to live—to work.

The Christian Sabbath

Work needed a counterpart, so God gave us physical rest. The tensions of our day so tax the spirit, soul, and body that God knew rest and renewal were essential factors in the preservation of the total person.

The whole of life—work and play—is to be lived under God and offered to Him in worship. But God knew we needed a special time set apart for Him to minister to us in a unique, special way. "Be still, and know that I am God" (Ps. 46:10). This is rooted in the life of God himself. After He labored six days in creating the universe, He rested!

Then God commanded:

"Remember the Sabbath day by keeping it holy. Six days you shall labor and do all your work, but the seventh day is a Sabbath to the Lord your God. On it you shall not do any work" (Exod. 20:8-10).

By making the Sabbath a means of physical and spiritual refueling, we elevate it to the plateau of privilege. We respect this day of leisure, for it gives an opportunity for the development of creative gifts and the expansion of the soul. It allows time for special prayer and worship.

Public Worship

While this includes private devotional practices, it also involves public worship. Jesus is again our model and example. He was always found in the synagogue on the Sabbath. His disciples set aside the first day of the week as the Christian Sabbath because that was the day Jesus rose from the dead.

One great Christian father made this comment, "There is no solitary Christianity." The fellowship and mutual encouragement of public worship is still vital to spiritual health. There is assurance and affirmation gained from joining faith with the family of believers. Many times a joint effort will turn defeat into victory and give power to the weak so they can persevere when otherwise it would be humanly impossible. God's Word has this to say:

55

"Let us not give up meeting together, as some are in the habit of doing, but let us encourage one another—and all the more as you see the Day approaching" (Heb. 10:25).

For those who fail to recognize God's wisdom in observing a day of rest and worship, there usually comes a time of reckoning. All too often these individuals not only suffer breakdown spiritually but also physically, mentally, and emotionally.

Know Your Limitations

As you continue to read through this section on health, hopefully you will find ways in which you can safeguard your bodily temple.

The Creator has given us physical laws of nature that we must respect. Failure on our part to obey them will eventually cause our bodies to send warnings that we should not ignore.

Stop

Let up

Relax

Rest

This means that we have exceeded our tolerance level. Our bodies could be nearing collapse!

Everyone wants a strong, healthy body. Illness and pain are no fun; being incapacitated is inconvenient; and our service to others certainly is limited. Too often we simply don't concern ourselves mentally about the preservation of the body. In fact, it's possible that some take better care of their material possessions than they do of their God-created physical bodies. What negligence! How unfair to themselves!

5

Nutrition and Health

The health and beauty of the face and the other parts of the body begins on the inside. Good nutrition is vitally important. This is why a proper balance of vitamins and minerals is essential if we are to look and feel our best.

For those who have not memorized the particular foods that provide the essential vitamins and minerals for feeding the body, here they are. *(See next page.)* They have been checked and approved by a competent nutritionist, a dermatologist, and an internist.

Minerals, the Foundation

Although there are 16 minerals that are essential to good health, 14 of these are usually gotten from a good balanced diet. Seldom do physicians recommend a supplement. *Iron* and *calcium* are the two minerals of which we are the most likely to be deficient.

Calcium

Calcium is considered one of the two most important minerals since it is the major builder of bones. The skeleton is constructed of living tissues composed of protein and minerals. Ninety-eight percent of the body's calcium is found in the skeleton. The teeth have 1 percent, and the other 1 percent is distributed throughout the body.

Calcium travels from the skeleton to supply a wide range of bodily needs. When the body is required to "borrow" calcium from the bones for a prolonged period of time without replacing calcium loss, the spine can suffer serious deterioration. Exercise is one of the best levelers. It can help retain a strong, healthy skeleton and retard demineralization.

The Contribution of Calcium to the Body

1. It is the major building material for healthy bones and teeth.

Vitamin Virtues

A — milk; liver; fruits—cantaloupe, apricots; spinach; leafy greens like broccoli, romaine; carrots and yams; pumpkin and squash

- resists infection
- most important aid to health of eyes
- assists in building strong bones, teeth, nails
- ensures the growth of new skin cells
- helps give the skin a glowing appearance (use with caution, can be toxic in large doses)

B — fish, liver, meat and poultry; milk; egg yolks; whole-grain breads and cereal; potatoes; oatmeal; tuna; leafy and dark green vegetables; mushrooms; corn; avocado; lima beans

- aids in growth, appetite, and digestion
- helps body utilize fat
- functions in maintenance of nervous system
- forms coenzymes used in the metabolism of all producing cells—particularly in the bone marrow where blood is produced

C — citrus fruit and juices; raw cabbage and green peppers; strawberries, melons, potatoes, and tomatoes; yellow and dark green vegetables

- aids the body's use of iron and calcium
- promotes development of strong teeth, gums and bones
- keeps skin from bruising easily
- protects vitamins A and E against oxidation
- builds collagen, the fibrous protein that holds skin cells together; gives the complexion a smooth, firm tone

D — sunshine; liver; canned salmon; egg yolk; butter

- aids in the transportation of calcium
- aids in growth, teeth and bones
- helps blood clotting
- aids in stabilizing the nervous system
- maintains heart action

E — oils such as peanut, soy and corn; wheat breads and cereals; egg yolk; liver; leafy green vegetables

- preservative and protector of cell membranes of all major organs
- aids in the formation of red blood cells as well as muscles
- guards against skin dryness
- may retard aging by slowing down the deterioration of cells

2. It is essential to erect posture.
3. It is used throughout the body for the regulation of muscles.
4. It helps prevent blood clotting.
5. It acts as nourishment for the body cells and nerves.

The calcium of our bodies is constantly moving in and out of the bones and needs daily replenishing. The loss of sufficient calcium can cause bones of the body to become brittle, breaking easily.

The Best Sources of Calcium

Dark green leafy vegetables
Citrus fruit and juices
Sardines, salmon, and oysters
Milk and milk products
Dried peas and beans
Sesame seeds

Iron

Iron deficiency, which often causes anemia, is considered the most prevalent nutritional problem in the United States today. It isn't difficult to detect it in people because they are usually pale in color, are often short of breath, and tire more easily than they should.

Its primary cause is that the average person absorbs only 10 percent of the iron derived from food. Although we retain much more from meat, fish, and poultry—20 percent—it drops to about 5 percent from vegetables. More and more people are going to fruit and vegetable diets, and this could be a major cause of the high rate of iron deficiency in our country today.

The Contribution of Iron to the Body
1. It assists in the metabolism of protein.
2. It's the major component of hair and nails.
3. It's involved in energy production.
4. It helps prevent dryness of the skin and gives color to the skin.
5. It's necessary for the proper functioning of the immune system.

The Best Sources of Iron

Liver (calves, chicken, beef)
Soybeans, navy and kidney beans
Bran flakes and whole grains

Sardines, oysters, lean meat
Dark molasses
Dark green vegetables

Sunshine, an Asset to Health

All of life's energy comes from the sun. So let's internalize sunshine with sun-kissed foods, such as fresh uncooked fruit and vegetables and nuts. Take advantage of them while they're in season—eat quantities!

They can play a vital part in destroying disease and restoring the ill body to full health again. This is why primitive people can be healthy by living off of nature's seeds, leaves, and even certain grasses. This is why some of our physicians from China, Japan, and Switzerland in particular encourage the use of products like herbs in doctoring the body naturally.

A doctor of my acquaintance suggested that a male patient of his lie in the sun a few hours every day to combat a severe case of hepatitis. The sun served as a healing tonic and stimulant for him. It was incredible how quickly he recovered. This doctor proved that sunshine can be one of nature's best means of healing. In addition, good food, proper rest, and positive mental hygiene were prescribed as top priorities for his patients.

However, dermatologists warn us about the irreparable damage that too much sun can do to the sensitive areas of the skin like the face, chest, and torso. They should always be protected with a good sunscreen (No. 15-No. 18). They also advise against ever lying in the direct sun between the hours of ten and two o'clock. *Sunburning is always to be avoided!* Patience is *crucial!* Begin by staying out only a few minutes at a time.

If your complexion can afford the luxury of the sun, let it minister to your body. The radiant energy of the sun will transmit and store life-giving elements in the body. It will counteract the artificial medication used so freely by many women today.

The Benefits of Fiber

"Let your food be a cure." This is an eye-catching advertisement recommending a "high fiber" diet. The phrase became more interesting as I made an extensive study concerning the benefits of such a diet. Because the foods are basic and encourage proper digestion

and elimination, it makes good sense. Of course, *anyone suffering from colon or digestive problems should consult with her physician before beginning any form of diet.*

However, it is high fiber foods that help to prevent such problems as:

chronic constipation
diverticulitis,
irritable bowels,
colon cancer,
spastic colon.

Specialists in the field of nutrition tell us that there are two kinds of fiber, soluble and insoluble.

Soluble fiber dissolves in water and forms a jellylike substance resembling pectin.

This is basically found in foods such as *beans, seeds, fruits, corn, and oats.*

Insoluble fiber does not dissolve in water but absorbs like a sponge.

The primary sources are found in bran from *whole-grain breads and breakfast cereals.*

Our fiber intake should range from 40 to 50 grams a day. But the average American diet provides only about 15 to 20 grams per day. This has resulted in intestinal problems for many people.

There should be no problem switching to such a healthful diet when many quality foods are high in fiber. There is also a plus. Instead of gaining weight you will actually lose! You tend to eat fewer calories because bulk makes you feel fuller.

In order to adequately enjoy the benefits from fiber you should eat regularly from each one of these five types:

- a variety of fresh fruit (some doctors have suggested that we should eat two whole fresh fruits such as a small apple, pear, or apricot daily). Eat any other fresh fruit you enjoy.
- a variety of fresh vegetables—especially potatoes with their skins, yams, carrots, broccoli, or corn.
- dried beans of all kinds, peas, and garbanzos.
- nuts, especially almonds. Go easy on nuts, they are high in calories (dry roasted cashews are the lowest).
- cereals—wheat, oats, rye, barley, buckwheat.

If you need more protein, brewer's yeast is one of the most energy-boosting foods available. It's a source of complete protein as well as containing all the elements of vitamin B complex. Try mixing it with V-8 juice or any unsweetened fruit juice. Some people add it to eggs, breakfast cereals, or various casseroles. Begin by taking only one-half teaspoon and gradually work up to two tablespoons a day.

What this "health diet" is basically suggesting is that we eliminate excess fat, oils, sugars, and salt. We eat natural foods instead.

There's nothing complicated—no hunger pangs; no danger to health—unless there is already a physical problem with the intestinal area. I repeat, be sure to talk with your doctor! He will guide you. But for the well person this can be a preventive step away from any such problems. This is a simple, sensible menu of natural health foods. Anything this good is worth a try!

High Fiber Recipes

Hopefully these recipes will encourage you to start on your "health diet" today. These are just a sample of what you can do with fiber foods.

Health Soup (serves 8-10)

6 carrots
1 large head cabbage
2 large onions
2 stalks celery
2 potatoes
1 large can tomato juice
2 c. beef broth
garlic powder and oregano
1 bay leaf
shredded cheese to garnish

Chop all vegetables. Simmer in enough water to cover. Cook until tender. Avoid overcooking. Add the remaining ingredients and simmer for 45 minutes. Remove the bay leaf before serving. Shred cheese over each serving.

Lima Bean Soup
(serves 6-8)

1½ c. dry lima beans
2 qts. water

3 stalks celery with leaves
1½ large onions
1 tbsp. chopped parsley
1½ c. chopped greens (spinach)
3 tomatoes
4 tbsp. corn oil
½ c. millet
¾ tsp. ground sage
1½ tsp. caraway seed
4 tbsp. brewer's yeast (optional)
½ tsp. nutmeg
2 tsp. thyme
½ tsp. fresh ground pepper
grated mozzarella cheese

Soak lima beans overnight in water. Chop the celery, onion, parsley, greens, and tomatoes rather coarsely. Place in large kettle with the lima beans, adding enough water to cover. Add the oil, millet, sage, caraway seed, yeast (if desired), and seasoning. Simmer 2 to

3 hours, adding water as necessary. Always keep the vegetables covered with water. Taste for seasoning and serve in individual bowls with grated mozzarella cheese (made from part skim milk) melted on top.

Chili Deluxe (serves 4)

2 tbsp. polyunsaturated vegetable oil
3 c. cooked soybeans, ground
1 large chopped onion
1 clove garlic, minced
1 tsp. oregano
1 tsp. cumin seed
6 tsp. chili powder
2 medium cans tomatoes
3 c. cooked soybeans, whole, or 3 c. cooked chili beans (or 1½ c. each)

In a large skillet combine fat, ground soybeans, onion, and garlic, and brown lightly. Transfer to large pot. Add oregano, cumin seed, chili powder, tomatoes, and whole portion of soybeans. Cook at least one hour.

Chicken and Rice Soup
(serves 8)

Cook one chicken with all fat and skin removed. Cool. Remove all remaining fat. To 7 c. of the chicken broth add the following:
1 c. brown rice
¾ c. wild rice (4 oz. package)
1 c. diced chicken
1 large bunch celery and leaves
1 extra c. celery leaves
1½ c. mushrooms, sliced
1 medium-sized potato, cubed
1 large green pepper, sliced

crushed red and black pepper to taste
2 large bay leaves
1 tsp. celery seed
¼ tsp. oregano
1 tsp. parsley, dried
1 tsp. spinach, dried
garlic and dried onions may be added, if desired
Cook slowly for 1½ hours. Top with croutons, if desired.

English Muffin Bread
(makes 2 loaves)

4-5 c. whole wheat flour
2 pkgs. active dry yeast
¼ tsp. baking soda
1 tsp. marjoram
½ tsp. thyme leaves
½ tsp. oregano leaves
2 c. skim milk
½ c. water
1 tbsp. apple juice concentrate
cornmeal

Combine 3 c. flour, undissolved yeast, baking soda, marjoram, thyme, and oregano. Combine milk and water in saucepan. Heat over low heat until liquids are very warm. Gradually add dry ingredients and beat well. Add apple juice concentrate. Stir in remaining flour to make a stiff batter. Transfer dough into two 8½" x 4½" x 2½" loaf pans (or 9" x 5" x 3" pans) that have been lightly greased and sprinkled with cornmeal. Sprinkle the tops of the loaves with additional cornmeal. Cover; let rise in warm place for 45 minutes. Bake at 400° for 25 minutes or until done. Remove from pans and let cool.

Chicken Breast Parmigiana
(serves 4)

½ c. oat bran
2 tbsp. whole wheat flour
1 tsp. oregano leaves
¼ tsp. pepper
2 chicken breasts, boned, split
1 egg, beaten
1 garlic clove, finely chopped
2 tbsp. polyunsaturated vegetable oil
1 8-oz. can tomato sauce
½ c. (2 oz.) shredded farmer cheese

Combine bran, flour, oregano, and pepper. Dip chicken in egg; coat with bran mixture. Sauté garlic and oil in large skillet. Add chicken; lightly brown. Add tomato sauce. Cover; simmer 15 minutes or until chicken is tender. Sprinkle cheese over chicken. Cover; continue cooking until cheese is melted. Serve over whole wheat spaghetti if desired.

Stuffed Zucchini (serves 6)

3 large zucchini
1 large onion, thinly sliced
1 green pepper, diced
1 clove garlic, minced
½ c. chopped fresh tomatoes
1 c. tomato juice
1 tsp. dried oregano
1 slice whole wheat toast

Cut the zucchini in half lengthwise. Scoop out the pulp, leaving ¼-inch-thick shells. Save the zucchini shells for stuffing. Dice the scooped-out zucchini; place it in a large nonstick skillet with the onion, green pepper, garlic, chopped tomatoes, ¼ c. of the tomato juice, and oregano. Cook until the vegetables are softened. Fill the zucchini shells with the cooked mixture and arrange in a baking dish. Pour the remaining tomato juice around the stuffed zucchini. Crumble the toast and sprinkle it on top of the stuffing. Bake at 350° for 30 minutes or until the shells are tender. Serve with the tomato juice gravy spooned over the shells.

Tomato Avocado Stuffed Salad
(serves 4)

4 large tomatoes
1 avocado, peeled and chopped
½ c. bran (oat)
½ c. chopped celery
2 tbsp. finely chopped onion
2 tbsp. chopped parsley
2 tbsp. lemon juice
¼ tsp. pepper

Slice ½ inch off top of each tomato. Remove pulp, reserving pulp and tomato tops. Finely chop; drain. Drain tomato shells. Combine pulp and tops with remaining ingredients. Spoon into tomato shells; chill until ready to serve.

Applesauce Bran Cookies

1 c. shortening
1 c. brown sugar
1 egg
1 c. golden applesauce
2 c. whole wheat flour
½ tsp. soda
½ tsp. salt
½ tsp. nutmeg
1 c. whole bran cereal
1 c. raisins

Cream shortening and sugar. Blend in egg and applesauce. Sift together flour, soda, and spices. Add to creamed mixture; mix well. Stir in bran cereal and raisins. Drop by teaspoonfuls on ungreased cookie sheets. Bake at 350° for 15 minutes. Makes about 3½ dozen cookies.

Croquettes à la King

Have cooking:
1½ c. raw brown rice cooked with 1½ c. bulgur wheat
Have ready:
⅔ c. dry soybeans, soaked overnight, cooked with 1 chopped onion, 1 bay leaf, and 1 tsp. poultry seasoning.
Croquettes
½ c. filberts
¼ c. cashews
1 c. walnuts
1 12-oz. can tomato paste (no salt added)
2 onions
1 c. whole wheat bread crumbs
2 tsp. corn oil margarine
Soybean mixture from above, mashed
2 eggs, well beaten
Wheat germ mixed with whole wheat bread crumbs (for rolling)

Chop first 6 ingredients finely with food chopper. Mix with margarine and mashed soybeans. (Mix should be quite moist; if not, add more tomato paste.) Form into baseball-sized balls and dip into beaten eggs. Roll in wheat germ and bread-crumb mixture. Bake at 400° for 30 minutes or until brown.

Sauce:
1 c. mushrooms, chopped
2 mushrooms, sliced
2 tbsp. beef broth
4 tbsp. margarine
2 tbsp. whole wheat flour
2 c. water

Sauté mushrooms in margarine. Add beef broth. Mix flour with a bit of water to make paste. Add to mushroom mixture. Blend on low burner. Gradually add water, stirring constantly. Bring to boil. Cook 5 minutes.

To serve:
Arrange rice and bulgur wheat mixture on serving platter. Place croquettes on top. Pour sauce over croquettes. Platter can be decorated with steamed asparagus or other green vegetables.

Dental Health

More and more medical doctors are working together with dentists in solving certain physical problems. They both confirm the fact that the mouth is often an indicator of health. This makes close attention to the care of teeth and gums one of the best "preventive medicines."

"Good genes have a definite influence on one's dental health. We inherit either a susceptibility or resistance to dental disease.

However, environmental factors are primarily responsible for the incidence of dental disease," according to Dr. Dennis Burgner who is a specialist in family dentistry.

"Nowhere is this more apparent than in the formation of cavities. Three factors must be present:

1. A susceptible tooth;
2. The presence of bacterial plaque on the tooth;
3. Sugar.

The 'sugar bugs' on the teeth use the sugar as food and produce acid. Within two to three minutes of exposure to sugar, the acid is strong enough to etch the tooth. The acid remains strong enough to attack the tooth for twenty minutes. With frequent exposure to sugar in the presence of bacterial plaque—a cavity is born!

"All three factors should be eliminated if cavities are to be avoided:

"1. The resistance of the tooth to acids should be increased by applying flourides—in toothpaste and/or in the dentist's office.

"2. 'Sugar bugs' should be eliminated by effectively brushing *and* flossing.

"3. Frequent exposure to sugar should be avoided, especially in-between-meal snacks. Mothers, you can monitor your children in this area.

"These common sense measures will go a long way toward controlling the formation of cavities and the maintaining of good dental health. Periodic professional cleaning and examination of the teeth by a dentist is also good insurance against serious dental problems."

Mothers' Responsibility

In a real sense the mother holds the key to her children's health. Young minds are fertile ground. They will grow whatever we plant. They are almost totally nondiscriminatory and will operate on what they are fed. This should say something to young mothers.

Stay alert and in control of the eating pattern of your children—even into the teen years. Creating an early appetite for sweets, salted foods, and carbonated drinks will be a habit difficult to break. Such foods can cause damaging effects in our adult years, even though we no longer indulge.

According to nutritionists, many children are overliquidated with milk because they haven't developed an appetite for vegetables, fruits, and meats. If children get hungry enough they will eat the proper food, provided they aren't given the option of filling their little "tummies" with liquids and sweets. Promoting the eating of quality food in proper portions during the maturing years will help to eliminate any cause for dieting, as such, at any age.

Mrs. Ethel Copeland, a nutritionist at a New York hospital and mother of four boys, testifies that in the beginning years she tickled the taste buds of her children with health foods. Junk diets never got a foothold with any of them. Today they are strong, well-developed boys—physically, emotionally, and mentally.

Children will eventually become what they eat! What they put in their mouths largely determines whether they are:

nervous or calm;

emotional or stable;

dense or alert;

weak or strong;

ill or healthy.

Mothers, keep that "health key" in your hands! Your children will love you for it as they grow older, even if their young minds fail to comprehend the wisdom of it now.

But the responsibility of the mother doesn't stop with the children. She influences her whole household. The health and well-being of her husband is also at stake. We can't always control everything the man in our life eats. But health foods can be prepared so attractively that they will create a desire for only the best. There have been far too many heart attacks among the husbands of our close friends to ignore the contributing factors—these all play a significant part:

overweight;

lack of exercise;

failing to cope with stress.

Physical Activity

Food intake must be balanced with energy output by exercising. Some healthy flexing of muscles around the house and yard could improve the emotional and physical well-being of hundreds of teenagers today. Too much leisure time is producing far too many dull minds and weak bodies among our children.

Physical exercise in some form is a basic requirement for proper development of the body. Even with children, failure to exercise tends to produce a sluggish digestion, flabby muscles, and inadequate elimination. Children who participate in a supervised health program will rarely fail to give proper attention to their bodies in adulthood.

Make a "hit" with your children! Be captain of the team—whatever the sport or exercise. Choose fun things they will enjoy—walking, bicycling, playing tennis, volleyball, golf, racquetball. Anything you do as a family unit can be good "health therapy" in more ways than one. It has been well said: "The family that plays together stays together."

6

The Role of Exercise—Nature's Tranquilizer!

Our bodies were designed to be physically active. Can't we accept exercise as a friend rather than an unpleasant discipline? Perhaps it will help if we are alerted to 14 rewards that we will receive from systematic exercising. It will:

- Improve the functioning of all the internal organs
- Clear the mind and calm the nerves
- Chase away tension, anxiety, and depression
- Banish extra pounds by controlling body fat
- Tone and firm our muscles
- Boost the energy level
- Increase self-confidence
- Suppress our appetite
- Help our bones last a lifetime
- Speed up our circulation
- Insure us against illness, including heart attacks
- Reduce aches and pains
- Aid in digestion and elimination
- Help us sleep more soundly

We can fit regular exercise into the busiest working day—if we don't think of it as a chore but as a refreshing break to help us feel more alert and energetic.

Six Common Excuses for Not Exercising Are:

1. *I can't spare the time for exercise.* If you have time to breathe and live—you have time to minister to your body.
2. *I'm too tired to exercise.* Fighting weariness is one of its benefits.
3. *It takes too long to work off a pound.* I'd rather diet! Firming and toning muscles are more beneficial than weight loss in many cases.
4. *Exercising will increase my appetite and I will eat more food.* It actually suppresses your desire for food. Test it!

69

5. *My exercise is gotten from doing my housework and running after children.* You need a change of scenery—fresh air; mental and emotional release; solitude and quiet.

6. *I'm too old to exercise.* No one is too old to gain a new lease on life. Individuals who engage in some program of regular exercise delay and reduce loss of muscle and bone mass.

Exercising also helps to retain cardiovascular functioning to a greater degree.

Designing our own health program eliminates any tendency to compete with someone else.

Living an active life as we grow older will help us remain alert mentally and physically. The more vitality, vigor, and stamina we possess, the longer we will be of use to the Lord. In consulting with doctors I have found they have without exception assured me that exercising will keep anyone younger longer.

The secret of any health program is to approach it with ease and sensitivity. Whether you are young or older, male or female, active or sedentary, your body deserves a gentle approach to sports and exercise. All athletic directors with whom I have conversed caution us about the consequences suffered by adults who go into crash programs of exercise.

Bodies that have been neglected for years cannot be rehabilitated in one week or even a month, any more than a mind that's been stagnant from the lack of intake can reverse itself overnight. Unless we are alert to "body language," sudden exercise that is too strenuous can easily do more harm than good.

Strained muscles and sore joints must be avoided. Easy does it! But let's do it! Let's allow the glow of our personal vitality to be the means of carrying the gospel of health to others.

Five Basic Principles

1. Check with your physician before entering any strenuous exercising program.

2. If there's a warm, diffused sensation, then you have adequately but not unduly exercised your muscles. This is considered "good healthy pain."

3. If your muscles at any time signal a sharp, focused sensation, it indicates "bad pain." You have overextended your endurance level in that particular area.

4. When you aren't feeling well your body is telling you something. Listen! Don't exercise at all—or modify what you're doing.

5. Competition in a health-exercise program is foolish. Needless injuries may occur. Working at your own pace is a better policy.

Water—a Prime Health Source

We live in a world of the woman athlete. More than at any other time in history women are participating in almost every active sport. Professional performers have been schooled in the value of water consumption. If they are to be at their peak in performance, they need the energy and endurance assistance that comes from water. They are also warned about the danger of dehydration.

The value of water in conjunction with exercise has never been questioned. However, it is essential that every mother be knowledgeable about the value of water and educate her children in this important subject. They may or may not be in active sports, but normal, active children can suffer water loss.

Of all *the essential nutrients, water is the most critical.* People have been known to survive as long as 10 weeks on their body's store of food. Without water, life would be over in a matter of days.

Try never to ignore thirst. Your body could be telling you that there is a water depletion. When we realize that every function of the body uses water, it's reasonable that an adequate water intake is vital.

Are you wanting to lose weight? Then why not take advantage of some foods that are high in water content, such as apples, celery, cucumbers, lettuce, bananas, tomatoes, spaghetti, lean meat.

The reason water is so vital to the whole body is that it (the body) is made up of 70 percent water. These "waterways" communicate oxygen and nutrients to the body, but they also transport waste from our bodies. Although some physicians feel it would be healthier if everyone drank some water 10 to 12 times a day, a minimum of 6 to 8 glasses daily is the basic recommendation. One advantage to drinking water is that it removes the temptation to "float our bodies" in coffee and carbonated drinks.

We have found out how essential water is internally. Now, let's look at some of the benefits water offers to us externally.

71

Water Exercising

Water offers the *single* best exercises. Almost anyone of any age can be a participant. You may have been injured; you may be "out of shape" physically; you may be overweight; you may never have exercised before. Yet, there is no reason why you should not thoroughly enjoy exercising in water. It will not only *firm* and *tone* your muscles but will relax them at the same time. Some women who have undergone hip or knee surgery have testified that water exercising was highly recommended by their surgeons. It proved to be an easy therapeutic treatment for *muscle-strengthening.*

It has been confirmed that we can *walk* two miles in four feet of water without incurring injury, muscle strain, or soreness of any kind. The reason is that water prevents the pounding, adverse effects of gravity caused by exercises like jogging, playing tennis, and the more strenuous sports.

Following an automobile accident where I suffered a severe whiplash and injury to the lower part of my back, three doctors recommended water exercises to help strengthen the injured areas. I can testify that water exercises really work!

Many more health spas for women are adding "exercising pools" to their basic exercising equipment. This is to accommodate the ones who have been unable to use much of their other equipment without discomfort.

Are you interested in such a program? Any health spa that has a pool will also have someone who will instruct you in a regularly scheduled program of water exercises.

Here is a complete set of Water Workouts. Try them! I know you will benefit from them.

Swimming

Swimming is to the '80s what jogging was to the '70s. I personally would not feel comfortable about patronizing public swimming pools. However, the pools in YWCAs and private spas for women provide facilities where you can swim to your heart's content.

It's not hard on your feet.

It's not injurious to your knees like jogging.

It's not an uphill pull like you encounter riding a bike.

It's not as strenuous as tennis.

It's not as damaging to your facial skin as jumping rope.

73

The only people who should not swim (specialists in the field of sports advise) are those who have neck problems. Raising your head out of the water as you do when you swim could put undue strain on any neck injured by a whiplash or similar injury.

Four Basic Benefits of Swimming Are:

1. **Arthritis** is helped through bobbing or swimming in water because the force on the joints isn't as great as when you are standing or walking. When you are in the water your weight is only one-tenth of what it would normally be. This makes bobbing up and down in water an excellent exercise for arthritic patients if they never actually swim. Jumping up and down forces the body against gravity and strengthens the joints, which is one of the sensitive areas of the arthritic person.

Water is also relaxing and helps keep the entire body more limber without being too strenuous on the muscles and joints.

2. **Heart therapy** is one of the specialties of swimming. Some patients have been advised to start a swimming program three weeks following a heart attack, indicating that it's a less strenuous exercise than most. It makes the heart stronger and can actually help prevent heart ailments.

3. **Stamina.** Swimming at least twice a week will keep one from tiring so easily. The secret is continuity. Swim close to the surface and don't waste energy spraying water with your arms and legs. You will tire less easily if you kick from the hips and let your knees bend slightly.

There is a difference between playing and really swimming. One will help you a little—the other a lot!

4. **Weight control** seems to be one of the popular topics for conversation these days. And swimming is one of the exercises that is recommended as an appetite suppressant. If anyone has a weight problem, diet alone simply does not do the job. Few, if any, ever successfully lose weight on any diet program without some form of exercise. For those who do lose, they have less than 1 chance out of 10 of keeping it off for a year.

There are some possible problems connected with swimming:
- Skin dryness
- Possibility of ear infections
- Allergic reactions to chlorine on skin, nose, sinuses, and eyes
- Back sufferers must avoid arching the back
- Neck injuries may be aggravated

Wearing goggles as well as a swim cap will help eliminate most irritations to the eyes and sinuses. Ear plugs may also be worn as a precaution against ear infections.

Walking for Exercise

The one major objection to swimming is that most people must leave home to exercise. This is why I prefer walking. I step out my door and take off!

Health walking is often more practical than more strenuous activities and just as beneficial. For instance, a brisk 30-minute walk can burn up to 300 calories—the same amount used up in 30 minutes of running or swimming.

Let your legs do the walking, not your fingers! It can be an invigorating way to open a day or a relaxing way to close it. Either time you will hear your heart, lungs, nerves, and head saying, "Thank you."

Our legs were not designed for the life of luxury to which many have become accustomed. They were attached to the body as a foundation to be used for locomotion. Placing one foot in front of the other provides us with one of the most complete, least expensive, and most thoroughly enjoyable exercises recommended by physicians today.

Many doctors are "walking examples" for their patients of the *vascular, respiratory,* and *psychological benefits* of walking. This is proof enough for me that it's a health habit.

Personally, I'm glad that most doctors are now saying, *"Walk, don't run!"* Watching joggers outside my dinette windows morning and evening has made me wonder if such torture is really good for one's health. The recent death of a 29-year-old professional football player who suffered cardiac arrest while jogging has confirmed my suspicion.

Rather than running the risk of suffering from shin splints, "runner's knee," and tight, overdeveloped muscles in the back of the legs—we can walk!

In observing women of all ages, I have noticed that some work at 100 percent capacity until they drop from sheer exhaustion while others suffer from "housewife" syndrome. In either case these women could use the therapy of walking. Ragged nerves can be soothed and boredom dissolved with regular exposure to fresh air.

This affirms at least one of the three primary benefits of walking—psychological uplift!

Walking as a family is a treat within itself. Rarely is there a need for parental coaxing. Children love getting out-of-doors.

- Walk to a park or to a lake; hike in the mountains.
- Let it be an education in nature—pick some wild flowers, gather a collection of small rocks, test each other on the names of trees, birds, flowers.
- Walking somewhere for breakfast on Saturday morning can be a delight.

These are experiences that will be etched on the memories of your children for a lifetime.

Walking as couples has many personal remunerations other than physical. You will relish the privilege of just being together and enjoying the beauties of nature. Your minds will be free of other things and you will find it easier to be sensitive to each other. Any problem or weighty discussion is off limits—a definite no-no!

By getting our husbands to put their legs into gear and walk briskly for 45 minutes to one hour, we will sense the tensions being released from their muscles and entire bodies. The increase of oxygen to their brains will give their spirits a lift, and we will have ourselves a "new man." That's reward enough for any special effort on our part.

Bonus Dividends:
- Posture improvement
- Slimmer hips
- Firmer stomach and arms (when walking, swing arms in rhythm with your legs)
- Improved waistline (reduction of inches is more important than weight loss)
- Leg strengthening
- General relaxing of the body

Create Your Own Program
(if you have any questions, consult your doctor before walking)

1. Begin at a more leisurely pace before working up to a brisk walk. There's no penalty for stopping occasionally. Take a few moments—breathe deeply, slowly. Then be on your way again!

2. The faster you walk the less time it will take to burn off

calories. Use a pedometer if you're serious about calculating the miles you travel. You can purchase one in any sports store.

3. If you're walking too fast to converse with someone, you are moving at too fast a pace. Slow down a bit and you will find yourself relaxing more.

4. Walk at least two miles a day if possible. If it's too much now, gradually work up to it.

5. Try to set an assigned time in your daily schedule for walking. Otherwise, it's difficult to remain faithful.

There are many other exercises that you may enjoy doing. I have mentioned only these few because they are the ones doctors have recommended as being the most beneficial as well as the most available to the average woman. The main thing is that we all do something!

Calisthenics

Since many women suffer with lower back problems I consulted with general practitioners, orthopedic specialists, and physical therapists to get their expert opinions as to the primary cause.

Without exception they said, "Strengthen the stomach muscles and you have solved one of the major problems with the lower back." Proper exercises and correct posture were two of the recommendations for remedying the problem.

Strengthening the stomach muscles will play a significant part in supporting the lower back. "Think of your spine as a telephone pole and your stomach and back muscles as guidelines," says Janet Couch, physical therapist at the Denver Presbyterian Hospital. "There must be a good balance," she continues, "between the muscles of the lower back and front of the spine. Unless the stomach muscles are strong enough to do their part adequately, too much pressure is forced on the lower back to maintain correct posture. Firm stomach muscles also help hold the pelvis in proper position." "If you have developed a sway back," says Dr. Holly Kitagawa, osteopathic surgeon and physician, "check your posture. It could be a contributing factor to your back problems." Stand and sit properly. Feel your stomach muscles become firmer as they pull you in. Then listen, I think you will hear your lower back saying, "Thank you."

Here is a set of exercises that were especially designed for helping to strengthen the stomach muscles. They should help to correct any imbalance between the stomach and lower back muscles.

1. **Standing reach**

Stand erect with your feet shoulder width apart and your arms extended over your head. Stretch as high as possible, keeping your heels on the ground. Slowly count to 15.

2. **Achilles stretch**

Stand facing a wall, two to three feet away. Lean into the wall with your arms extended. Move your left leg forward one-half step or more. Lower your right heel to the floor. Lower your body toward the wall, stretching your heel tendon in the right leg. Slowly count to 5 or 10. Reverse leg position and repeat, performing exercises 3 to 6 times on each leg.

3. **Seated pike stretch**

Sit on the floor with your legs extended and your knees together. Exhale and stretch forward slowly, sliding your hands down to your ankles. Try to touch your kneecaps with your chin, keeping your legs as straight as possible. Hold position. Slowly count to 5 or 10. Return to your starting position, inhaling deeply. Repeat 4 to 6 times.

4. **The dove**

Stand with your feet apart, legs slightly bent, and your hands clasped behind your back. Slowly bend at the waist while elevating your arms behind your back to the "stretching point." Slowly count to 5 or 8. Relax and repeat.

5. **Flexed-leg back stretch**

Stand erect with your feet shoulder width apart and your arms at your sides. Slowly bend over, touching the ground between your feet. Keep your knees relaxed and flexed. Slowly count to 20 or 30. Note: If at first you can't reach the ground, touch the top of your shoe line. Repeat 5 times.

6. **Supine hip rotations**

Lie flat on your back with your legs together and your arms away from your sides, palms down. Pull your knees toward your chest and rotate your hips and legs to the left until they are touching the floor. Keep your shoulders and back flat. Repeat 2 to 4 times on each side.

7. **Double knee pull**

Lie on your back with your feet extended and hands at your sides. Pull both of your legs to your chest, lock your arms around your legs, and pull the lower part of your back slightly off the ground. Hold and slowly count to 30 or 40. Repeat 7 to 10 times.

8. **Alternate knee pull**

Lie on your back with your feet extended and hands at your sides. Pull one leg to your chest, grasp with both arms, and slowly count to 5. Repeat 7 to 10 times with each leg.

SECTION III

The Whole Woman—
Mentally and Emotionally

7

Mental and Emotional Health

It is impossible to separate the mind and emotions from the body. All three are linked together in the total personality. Each affects the others. *An unhealthy body seriously influences our thoughts and our feelings.* Then, as we shall see, the mind controls the body, and often poor thought patterns can result in psychosomatic (mentally induced) illness. On the other hand, numerous specialists in the field of stress, including the School of Medicine in the Department of Microbiology at Pacific Northwestern Research Foundation, feel that *a positive mental attitude coupled with a love for self and others can ward off 70 percent of all illnesses.*

Since *the body is the servant of the mind,* the mind must become sensitive to "body language." This is the only way that the mind and body can learn to work together as a unit. It means that *when your emotional radar goes up—listen!* It's a warning that something is interfering with the proper functioning of the body. Physical distress of any kind can be a form of body language cautioning the mind to act.

Any woman suffering from severe nervous and emotional problems should not hesitate to seek competent professional help. We shall be dealing primarily with basic principles of "preventive medicine" and positive, constructive ways in which we may cope with some problem areas.

Mental Hygiene

Jesus' mind was a model for ours. If we are to follow this pattern we will have to study the mind of Christ so we can imitate it. This is a big order! Let's observe some of the obvious characteristics of His mind.

1. It was an illuminated mind

The Holy Spirit was at home in His heart and clarified and enlightened His mind. *Dr. Adam Clarke,* a commentator and one of the great Bible scholars of his day, has *testified that after the Holy Spirit took possession of his own mind he could learn more in one day than he previously could in a week.* This is reason enough to allow God to control and to bring into captivity our every thought. Nothing else can more effectively quicken our mental powers and reasoning faculties.

2. It was an instructed mind

Luke 2:52 tells us that "Jesus grew in wisdom" as well as in physical stature. He used every means possible to cultivate His mental abilities. We too must give serious attention to the development of our God-given intellects. Just as weeds come up in an untended garden, so *unhealthy thought patterns will grow in carelessly kept minds.* "Study to shew thyself approved unto God" (2 Tim. 2:15, KJV).

3. It was a pure mind

Jesus' heart was clean and it was only natural that He would have pure thoughts. But He constantly guarded against the temptation to let His mind move in the wrong direction. Spirit-filled women dare not take the maintaining of mental purity lightly. Any attacks in this area by Satan must be firmly resisted.

4. It was a humble mind

Humility is the *queen of all virtues.* Who personified it more beautifully than our Savior? When He gave the eight beatitudes in the Sermon on the Mount, He put humility first (Matt. 5:3). It is *the grace for which grace is given.*

5. It was a noble mind

All of the above combined to produce nobility in the mind of the Master. And we may "Let this mind be in you [us], which was also in Christ Jesus" (Phil. 2:5, KJV).

Negativism

One of the greatest contributors to poor mental health is negative thinking. Holiness Christians are not immune from this malady. In fact, all too many sanctified women have associated the "thou shalt nots" of the Ten Commandments and contemporary rules for holy living with a predominantly negative life-style. Christianity should speak positive enthusiasm! Jesus made it clear in His Word that He came to bring abundant life, not a limited life. *Holiness is wholeness!* It reserves no place for negative thinking.

One of the best ways to combat negativism is to eliminate from our mental and verbal vocabulary such words as

- Cannot
- Unworkable
- Impossible
- Inconceivable
- Hopeless
- Unthinkable
- Insurmountable
- Unattainable

Drs. Norman Vincent Peale and Robert Schuller have proved that there is unlimited power in positive, possibility thinking. The use of *an affirmative, uplifting vocabulary* in both our thoughts and spoken words *will work wonders in promoting good mental hygiene.*

The finest therapy for negative thinking is given to us in God's Word. It is guaranteed to counteract and cure mental negativism. If you have been troubled by this problem, take this prescription:

> "Whatever is true,
> Whatever is noble,
> Whatever is right,
> Whatever is pure,
> Whatever is lovely,
> Whatever is admirable
> —if anything is excellent or praiseworthy
> —think about such things" (Phil. 4:8).

Mental depression often comes as a result of emotional dejection and sadness. It's usually accompanied by a lack of interest in activities involving other people. These individuals also tend to think too much about themselves both physically and mentally. In talking with others, their minds seem to dwell more on the past than on the present. Even close friends become less important, and they hesitate to meet and make new friends.

Mental depression is often transferred to physical symptoms. If the nervous condition brings the focus of attention on the stomach and bowels, such symptoms as nerve spasms, constipation, and diarrhea may occur. Peace of mind is usually impossible unless these individuals recognize their condition of depression.

Healthy Emotions

"Don't get emotional!" We've all said it and heard it. The truth is, we don't *get* emotional—we *are* emotional. God made us that way with feelings such as joy and sorrow and love and anger. *Emotions are a vital part of one's personality. They add seasoning to the diet of daily living.* Wouldn't life be boring without them?

Do you experience both elevated and depressed moods? Of course! We all do. Why do you think the Psalmist said, "Why art thou cast down, O my soul? . . . hope thou in God" (Ps. 42:11, KJV). Do you want calmness and peace? Then learn to wait for the tide to come in. Soon the turmoil and confusion will pass. *Quietness and serenity cause you to rest in the Lord.*

A Christian psychiatrist was very frank and almost blunt with one of his patients one day. This person happened to be a gifted and popular Christian worker. "Is it possible," the doctor said, "that you are nearing a collapse emotionally and physically? The Lord has been good in giving you more spiritual and natural gifts than the average person. But He has also given you a brain—use it! No one can expect to live with an overtaxed body for long periods of time without suffering the consequences, both physically and emotionally."

"This is good advice for all Christians who drive their 'machinery' too long without coming in for a check-up, for repairs and, if necessary, a complete overhauling," responded an associate who was standing nearby. Furthermore, Dr. Morris Fishbein, editor of the *Medical Encyclopedia,* warns that emotions are more far-reaching than visible evidence usually indicates. Although there are different forms of emotions and our bodies react differently to them, he feels that *any emotion, mild or severe, registers in every cell and tissue of the body.*

Look at this report made in 1978. It was estimated that there were *450,000 Americans who died of sudden cardiac arrest.* After spending years and millions of dollars researching a remedy for high blood pressure, cancer, and heart problems, physicians are still debating the causes of these dreaded diseases. However, there is a growing number of cardiologists who agree that *stress brought on by undue pressure and emotional upsets is becoming recognized as the number one contributing factor in all three of the top "killers" today.*

These cardiologists feel that the best approach to finding a *remedy is to examine the mental attitude and emotional state of these patients* in such basic areas of their lives as

- home relationships
- job involvements
- social obligations

Where there is happiness and harmony in the major areas of a person's life, there is more apt to be a relaxed body, mind, and emotions. This relieves negative stress that takes its toll on the functioning of the body.

Our emotions must be carefully understood and monitored if they are to function properly and usefully. For example, *Christians can't "go by feeling." We live by faith.* Then our feelings will follow along. This is the correct order. First John 3:21 tells us that the final test of our relationship to God is not what our emotions say but what our spirits testify: *"If our hearts do not condemn us, we have confidence before God"* (italics mine).

In every area of life, *emotion must be disciplined so that it becomes a useful servant* rather than a dominating master. Drugs are a good example of this principle. Millions of people, both young and older, are caught in tragic addiction to narcotics. The underlying cause is a commitment to feeling good, however that may be achieved. Marijuana, cocaine, heroin, and a host of other drugs are the means of reaching a "high." The terrible aftereffects are a dreadful price to pay for an emotional lift. Hopefully no one reading these words will ever go to this extreme, but all of us need to exercise deliberate caution in the proper discipline of our emotions.

Accept Your Emotional Limitations

God never demands the impossible from us. The sooner we accept this fact and live our lives accordingly, the better off physically we will be. *We aren't "Superwomen," so let's not make an attempt to be!*

Those who have experienced severe emotional problems would do well to read Dr. David Seamand's excellent book, *Healing for Damaged Emotions.* This evangelical pastor approaches the subject from a very practical viewpoint and provides some very helpful solutions that are both spiritually and professionally valid.

Health and Stress

Any discussion of physical, mental, and emotional wholeness is not complete without a study of the subject of stress and its relationship to the total personality.

Let's look at some of the symptoms of stress; some of the causes and proven solutions.

Stress and Distress

Medically, stress has been defined as the degree of damage caused by the daily wear and tear of life. Each time anyone encounters intense exertion, bodily injury or disease, emotional crisis or mental trauma, the body experiences a certain degree of physical or psychological disturbance. Everyone sooner or later is going to encounter stress to some extent. There's no way to avoid it because the world is full of stressful situations.

Since the beginning of the 1980s the word *stress* has become a household word.

> Stress—the No. 1 killer
>
> Stress—the "Great White Plague" of the 1980s
>
> Stress—the greatest destroyer of human health and well-being
>
> Stress—the emotional damage caused from everyday living

Yes, stress seems to be a devastating calamity that has invaded our nation today. It's like a fever, and the degree of temperature varies with the degree of infection. As we move through the next few pages, let's examine our own lives as Christians to be sure we're not sucked into the "stress vacuum."

All human emotions, love as well as hate, involve some degree of stress. And normal emotional stress is healthy. Without reasonable stress we wouldn't even be alive. That's what keeps our bodies going and our lives productive. For instance, who would want to live a completely colorless existence where we never experienced a responsiveness to excitement or challenge or love, all of which exert some stress.

Most of us can cope with psychological pressures and emotional stress, such as being pushed for time or meeting public demands, if we know they are temporary. It's when we can't see the end in sight that it has a tendency to bring about emotional and mental disturbances. This is when stress becomes destructive and chronic.

Stress also becomes hazardous to our health when there develops a strong and persistent mental and emotional conflict, which in turn may trigger physical problems. Both psychiatrists and other doctors agree on this. Is it any wonder that some medical authorities believe that 70 to 80 percent of all illness is caused, directly or indirectly, by emotional upsets.

Many people have searched for years trying to locate someone in the medical field who could perform a "miracle cure" for destructive stress. A surgeon might use a scalpel to eliminate the results of prolonged stress, but he can't cut stress out of our lives.

Donald D. Fisher, M.D., made an intensive study of all his women patients who had breast cancer during a one-year period. He found that without exception each one had gone through a traumatic emotional experience that he feels could have contributed significantly in activating the cancer cells within her body. Dr. Fisher implies time and time again that most of our illness is not the result of some determined, destructive disease, but rather a type of battle fatigue that results from our contact with the social world. Jess Lair, Ph.D., feels basically the same way. He sees sickness not as an enemy from the outside, but rather as a breakdown in our internal defenses. We are too tense, too uptight, too unrelaxed!

Far too many good people are giving their lives, perhaps prematurely, because of the dreaded disease of cancer as well as heart attacks, strokes, and perforated ulcers and colons. There is evidence that all are connected directly or indirectly with stress, tension, and pressure. We must fight against this enemy that is invading and destroying the bodies created to be well and strong and useful for God.

Our responsibility lies in learning to handle what is commonly known as positive stress before it becomes negative or harmful. A positive attitude and reaction toward pressure or undue tension will help us develop a proper sense of control. That means we will accept it mentally! Consequently we will prevent stress from affecting the vital organs of our body. This is crucial! For if and when we allow stress to become sustained and unrelieved over a long period of time, it lowers the resistance of the body. This makes it vulnerable to all kinds of psychosomatic illnesses that often shatter the nervous system says neurologist John B. Woodard of Denver.

It has been suggested by medical groups that we pinpoint everything in a stressful situation that bothers us—then, imagine ourselves successfully handling the event. Remember, no one does anything to us inwardly unless we allow it. As long as we are a part of the human race we will suffer some unpleasant experiences. But if we remain in control of our inner feelings and allow God to take charge, He will act as our defense. So we relax in His power and strength. We let fly out of the window every stressful, fretful, or fearful feeling with which Satan tries to defeat us. God has given us a free will. *It's up to us to make our wills His will*—in all things. That means allowing His strength and relaxation to be ours internally as well as externally.

A district superintendent had been through a very distressing situation with one of the churches under his jurisdiction. He made an appointment with General Superintendent Dr. Hardy C. Powers in an attempt to find a solution.

"Dr. Powers, I think I'm going to have a nervous breakdown," was the opening remark made by the ministerial leader. Dr. Powers looked at him for a moment, then gave him God's formula for solving problems.

"If you feel it would help to have a breakdown, go ahead and have it! But please drive out to the country behind someone's barn where no one will know. Then, come home and *face your situation with God as your defense. Trust Him!* The problem wasn't of your making and you cannot solve it. Only God can do that! Make yourself available as His human instrument and the problem will be solved."

The district leader didn't have his breakdown, but through the power and leadership of Christ the problem was solved. And it solved one of his own personal problems at the same time—how to handle stress. Philippians 4:6 advises us not to be anxious about anything. *If God is in charge, victory is assured.* Not always immediately, but ultimately!

God in His act of creative genius made these physical bodies of ours complex but remarkably durable. He knew the abuse they would have to endure from well-meaning but sometimes careless people like you and me. *Each time we allow our bodies to be attacked by undue pressure, tension, and stress, our total health is in danger.* So if any of us need to change our life-style in order to add some happy, productive, and healthy years to our lives, the Great Creator is waiting to help us do just that!

Are we allowing personal relationships to disturb us? *Stressful encounters with others can take their toll on us physically and mentally*—but *only if we allow them to govern our thinking, emotions, and priorities.* God wants to set us free from getting under bondage to anyone who would keep us from being at our best for Him. Many times problems arise as a result of being "people pleasers" rather than "God pleasers." Haven't you found out by now that it's literally impossible to keep in perfect step with everyone— try as you will? Perhaps it's because we are all individuals with different ideas and goals and dreams. As long as we are honoring and pleasing God He will take care of us when there are those who fail to understand what we do, when we do it, and why we do it. It will make little difference to some whether we say yes or no—it will be wrong. Jesus certainly was not exempted from such encounters. But He came out victoriously, and so will we. He can and will keep us relaxed in mind and spirit when our eyes are fixed on Him.

Here is a recommended formula for successful daily living:

- Begin each new day with our spiritual bodies in good health with nourishment and guidance from the Lord.
- Trust God to help in keeping our priorities in proper balance.
- Keep our schedule in harmony with His timetable.
- Try to avoid stressful situations. Or if they do arise, believe God for enough love and understanding to keep you relaxed and in complete control of your emotions.

Let's look at some suggested ways that have helped many people combat undue stress and pressure:

Don't Overcommit Yourself

Learn to say no when it's appropriate. There's a limit to everyone's mental and physical endurance—even yours! You can't possibly please everyone, so why try? Seek God's direction and speed. "He knows your frame."

Be Sensitive to "Body Language"

If your body is sending you warning signals, you have a physical problem. Don't ignore them. Have the symptoms diagnosed immediately. Then work to avoid in the future any undue emotional and mental strain that brought on your symptoms.

Balance Work with Play

Apply yourself each day until you have a sense of godly accomplishment. Then balance your schedule with the fourfold plan practiced by Jesus himself: Besides working, He worshiped, rested, and relaxed. He functioned at the peak of His capabilities. So can we live a balanced life.

Reserve Some Time Each Day Just for Yourself

Loaf a little—relax! Re-create your mind, your body, your spirit; laugh, read, exercise, pray, worship. You will be of more value to yourself, to God, and to everyone around you for having done it. And *don't go on a guilt trip while you're doing it.* You deserve it!

Determine the Amount of Rest and Sleep That's Adequate for You

We all want to feel good and operate at our best. That means we set the alarm to fit our bodily need. God did not mass produce us on an assembly line. We were individually created. That gives you the only human "power of attorney" over your own body, mind, and emotions. Act on it! Everyone (including ourselves) likes us better when we've had enough rest and sleep.

Learn to Accept What You Cannot Change

Some circumstances are beyond our control. Don't fret or worry about them. Trust God to make you an overcomer. He's a master at this! Commit every need and every situation to the only One who is able to make all things work together for our good and His glory.

In Conclusion

Satan is out to brainwash anyone he can. Let's not allow it to happen to us. We must stay in control of our minds and thus condition our bodies and emotions. Refuse to submit to destructive pressure, tension, and stress.

Serving Christ cannot give us insurance against stress-producing situations. But God specializes in taking the most devastating situations and turning them into spiritual triumphs as He glorifies His name in our lives. Knowing this, can we accept the fact that every trial and circumstance—even distressful situations—could be a way of God's measuring our faith in and dependency on Him?

If God does not choose to divinely touch and heal a particular mental or emotional need, than seek professional help! This need not hamper our faith in the Great Physician. Both prayer and medicine are fighting the same disease. Knowing that God fully understands our needs is the most therapeutic factor in our healing.

Are you willing to go on a crusade with me to fight any stressful obstacle that would stand in the way of total health? No matter how major, every problem has within itself the seeds of its own solution. It may necessitate readjusting some attitudes and developing strategies for dealing with some sticky situations. But where it's needed, let's do it!

The real secret of freedom from stress is to "cast all your anxiety on him because he cares for you" (1 Pet. 5:7). Give Him plenty of time to work. He is still "able to do immeasurably more than all we ask or imagine, according to his power that is at work within us" (Eph. 3:20).

Diet and Stress

Unbelievable as it seems, one's diet can actually assist in coping with stress—or it can aggravate the problem. According to Vernon R. Young, Ph.D., professor of nutritional biochemistry at the Massachusetts Institute of Technology, the body goes through a loss of nutritional reserve—especially in vitamins A and C—anytime one is under severe stress. If we can avoid altogether or lessen anything destructive to our bodies by controlling our diet, then let's be smart enough to do it.

Here are a few protective foods that are recommended to combat pressure, tension, and stress:

PROTEIN—especially milk products because they contain riboflavin and calcium

VITAMIN A—found in dark green vegetables such as spinach, romaine, broccoli; and items in the yellow vegetable family like carrots, squash, and sweet potatoes

VITAMIN C—present in citrus fruits; baked potatoes; strawberries; tomatoes and green peppers

Are you guilty of keeping salted nuts, cookies, chocolates, potato chips, etc., handy to your fingertips for a quick energy lift? If so, doctors tell us why this is not a wise practice. Sweets actually make our blood sugar rise and fall so quickly that they leave us feeling more weary than before. Salty foods tend to make us feel bloated and uncomfortable because we retain too much liquid.

Then there's the coffee break! We have all read the warnings concerning caffeine beverages such as coffee, tea, hot chocolate, and some soft drinks. It's possible that caffeine can increase a nervous-system imbalance, especially when you add something sweet along with your beverage. The two actually add up to a stress-producer rather than a relaxer. Take the break, but drink a large glass of water instead. Did you know that water will actually give you an energy lift? If you must have something with flavor, try fruit juice. It's another health drink.

Exercise—a Natural Tranquilizer

If you want a natural tranquilizer, try exercising. It can increase the amount of carbon dioxide in your blood. Remember how tense your neck and shoulders become after sitting at a desk studying, typing, or writing? Or how about standing at the ironing board for an hour or cleaning house or teaching in a classroom? What's needed is an exercise to relieve the tension in the upper part of your body; an exercise that will help relax tight muscles. Try these:

Deep Breathing

Unless necessary it's advised that we never sit more than two hours straight without a break.

Walk around or stand while you inhale deeply through your nose. Breathe deeply enough to fill your entire chest and abdominal cavities. Hold for a count of 10, then exhale slowly through your mouth. Repeat three or four times. You can actually feel the tension going from your body. It helps to resolve stress and disharmony between mind and body.

Head Rolling

This is an exercise commonly known to further relax the upper part of your body from tense muscles.

Drop your head on your chest, then slowly turn it as far to the right side as possible. Let your head drop backward, completely relaxed. Hold for a moment. Then move your head around to the left side and slowly bring your head back to an upright position. Repeat as often as it takes to feel perfectly relaxed.

Stretching

One simple stretching exercise will coordinate mind, body, and action.

Stand straight and reach toward the sky with both arms, inhaling as you look upward, exhaling as you slowly lower your arms to your sides and your head to an upright position. It will stretch your spine and allow air to come in between your vertebrae and ribs.

Much of the stress in your life can be brought under your control. By following the simple rules outlined in this chapter, hopefully you can convert yourself into a less distressful personality.

8

Laughter—Nature's Best Medicine

"God has brought me laughter,
and everyone who hears about this
will laugh with me."
(Gen. 21:6)

Laughter is a natural expression of joy, excitement, amusement, mirth. Although it's usually an emotion expressed by an explosive, inarticulate sound of the voice, it's possible to laugh with the countenance and eyes when no audible sound is heard.

In Eccles. 3:4 we are told that there is an appointed time for everything—"a time to weep and a time to laugh." There's a real possibility that *those who have not learned to laugh may spend too much time weeping.*

Gertrude, a minister's wife who had walked through a deep valley of sorrow and disappointment, said to her mother, "I certainly have nothing to laugh about these days!" Her wise mother responded, "Then, daughter, *try laughing at yourself! It might help loosen you up a bit.* Discouragement is one of Satan's most powerful weapons; don't let him use it on you. Start praising the Lord for your blessings. You will soon find something for which you can be joyful."

In Gen. 21:6 Sarah said, "God has brought me laughter, and everyone who hears about this will laugh with me." Isn't that beautiful? God wants us to laugh because it's contagious! Our world is hungry for the sound of it. Not laughter that comes from sinful living, but the ring of praise and joy and gladness from a heart that's filled with God's love. So *be happy; it will bring laughter and happiness to someone else.*

Statistics show that almost *20 million people living in the United States are suffering from some degree of depression and emotional disorders.* Laughter would lift the spirits of the majority of these people—not superficial, but joyful laughter that comes from the heart. I have seen it cushion pain and disappointments that have entered the lives of some unexpectedly and uninvited. I have seen problems seem less tragic because that person was able to laugh. Since it's a prescription ordered by medical doctors today that's free and has no bad side effects, why don't we take advantage of their expert advice? Of course, God's Word is full of the same prescription. It's yours for the taking. We have only to follow the example of Jesus. I believe He enjoyed life; that He had a real sense of humor; that He was not stingy with His smiles. And rather than taking away from His ministry of love, this enhanced it. It drew people to Him. God will help it do the same for us—inside our homes as well as in the outside world.

Dr. Donald Fisher suggests that *the number one health hazard in today's world could be the unhappy situations found in the home.* The number two hazard is in the area of occupation. Actually, this is often what places marriage in first place. If a person works under stress on the job, that occupational stress takes a detour through the marriage relationship. Keeping a chuckle near the surface of our personality could play a part in relieving the pressure from people on the job who so often "bug" us.

Too many people too much of the time are attempting to swim upstream. They must speed things up, help things along! They could easily carry around with them a sign that has become well known among impetuous, eager, and sometimes overzealous Christians. *"God, give me patience. And please—hurry it up, will You!"*

One specialist speaking on stress projected that 7 out of every 10 patients who walk into a doctor's office this year could save themselves pain, time, and money if they would only

- smile instead of frowning;
  - be optimistic instead of negative;
    - be happy instead of disgruntled;
      - exercise faith instead of doubting.

Can you imagine the transformation that would take place in the world today, this year, if every professing Christian would follow such a philosophy of living!

Grace looked at her four-year-old son, John, and said, "Smile." Then she used the phrase that Robert Schuller has made so popular, "God loves you and so do I." "Well, I don't love nobody and I don't want to smile," he said as he continued to scowl. A friend who was visiting Grace questioned her child psychology. "Don't you think it's hypocritical to teach your child to smile on the outside when he's feeling unhappy on the inside?"

"No, not really," Grace replied. "What do you think Jesus meant when He suggested that when we pray and fast we wash our faces before 'going out'? I believe God wanted us to present to the world a cheerful countenance that speaks of the love of Christ. Hopefully my children will learn this lesson while they are young."

What a beautiful challenge and influence for all mothers to exert in the home before their families. If we must sigh or moan or complain, let's restrict it to a secret place of prayer where only God will hear. This will give us a chance to transfer all the frustrations that are pulling smiles from our faces to Christ. This will prove to our world that His peace is stronger than any agony of pain and grief that Satan can bring our way.

And don't stop with smiling; laugh! Laugh heartily several times a day whether you feel like it or not. This will prevent stress from entering your bodies in a destructive manner. If you are in doubt, listen to this story.

A woman in her sixties was admitted to the hospital with severe abdominal pain and vomiting. For months she had tried to ignore the warning signals that had been flashing on and off from her body. But she held a responsible position, you see, and didn't know how the office could possibly function without a manager. Isn't it interesting how we feed our ego by thinking we're indispensable?

Now she had just been given the verdict—inoperable cancer! What a devastating blow. She had so much of life ahead of her. So much that she had not accomplished. What was she to do? She had no husband, no family. Was she to give up, let go of life because of a few words voiced by a doctor? "Three, six, nine months at the longest," he said.

Suddenly she went down memory lane to something their family doctor had said years ago. "Laughter is the best medicine for sweeping out our insides," he had said. "Laugh, chuckle, giggle—I don't care how you do it, just do it! Not once, but often during the day. If bad emotions can cause stress, then good emotions can counteract it."

She suddenly realized that all too often during her adult life laughter had not been practiced as a daily exercise. She had not intentionally left God out of her race to achieve, to win, to excel. But she had. God could have kept her relaxed. He could have kept any emotion or stress detrimental to her body from becoming destructive.

Again she thought about the doctor's words, "Laughter is the best medicine for sweeping out our insides." What did she have to lose? She would start sweeping today!

She picked up the telephone and started calling her friends. She didn't explain why, she simply made a request that they come and visit her in the hospital at a certain time on a particular day. "And," she said, "please bring a notebook filled with your most hysterical jokes and stories. You are to make me laugh until you turn my insides upside down." And they did! After her friends got her started she continued on her own. Several times every day she would read a book, listen to a radio or television program, or visit with someone in person who would make her laugh until the tears would roll freely down her face.

In three months she made her specialists in the field of medicine look bad professionally. They are probably still unable to believe that a period of hearty laughter several times a day could cure cancer. But according to her testimony it did. She is a firm believer that laughter is nature's way of sweeping from our "insides" every emotion hazardous to our health.

Do you feel that this has to be an isolated case; that it could never happen again? Here is another situation almost identical to the one mentioned above.

Norman Cousins, the longtime editor of the *Saturday Review,* entered a New York hospital suffering from a very serious illness. He was given the only treatment known to medical science for this ailment. It failed to cure him, and he finally checked himself out of the hospital.

Mr. Cousins had heard about the medicine of "laughter." He decided to experiment! What could he lose? So moving into an apartment near the hospital, he began doctoring himself with the therapy of laughter. He bought a number of old films of such comedians as Laurel and Hardy and the Marx Brothers. Each day he took time to watch and listen to these films.

This resulted in several hours of hilarious laughter daily. He began to feel better and his symptoms started to disappear. The hospital monitored his progress with real interest. His physicians were forced to admit that healing was taking place. After several months he was declared totally cured and returned home to live a normal life.

Am I suggesting that every cancer patient can be cured with laughter? No, definitely not! If that were true we would have several thousand people finding some reason to laugh hysterically in order to cure themselves. Nor am I indicating that all cancer is the same— or induced by stress. I *am* passing on to you what many medical men and women are discovering about negative stress and the destructive effect it can and is having on people, mentally and physically.

People by nature are not depressed or bored or stressful. They get that way because they need laughter as a leveler. This makes laughter mandatory for good health, not an elective.

If you tire easily and desire more energy, then relax and enjoy the therapeutic value of laughter and play. You will have more stamina for serving the Lord because your mind and body will not be tense, rigid, or nervous. I can guarantee that people will like you better as a relaxed person, and your productivity in every area of your life will greatly improve.

Medical experts believe that there's healing power in a hearty laugh—so do I!

The Face Reflects Stress

The face reflects how we feel on the inside as well as on the outside. If we want the glow of God's love shining through our countenance; if we want to look and feel fresh and vibrant and alive; then, let go of stress!

- Pressure and tension can change one's mental outlook.
- Negative attitudes and feelings of low self-worth can be reflected through the eyes, expression, and voice.
- Sleepless nights will make us feel and look fatigued.
- Existing skin problems such as acne, psoriasis, or atopic eczema can be aggravated.
- Stress encourages furrowed brows, worried expressions, wrinkled foreheads, a "turned down" mouth—all resulting in a drawn look of the face that speaks of unhappiness.

The world is looking for peace and joy and happiness in our faces. We do not dare misrepresent who Jesus is and His promise of deliverance. He knows our level of stress tolerance. Our health and happiness is His business. No situation will go beyond His control—thus our control.

9

The Power of Color

A simple change of colors has been known to lift a person from a state of depression to a plane of activity, creativity, and happiness.

The daughter of a Baptist minister shared the story of her father's death and her mother's dampened spirit of dejection.

"Ever since I can remember," she said, "my mother had worn brown-, black-, and beige-colored clothes. I had always longed to see her dress in colors that were cheerful, soothing, exciting—anything, in any color, just so it had life to it!

"Finally, knowing that something must be done to lift Mother out of her deep depression, I took her to a color analyst. You would not believe the transformation! Color brought about a whole personality change in Mother. For the first time in her life she became a 'colorful' person. Her self-confidence soared. People complemented her on how well she looked; her complexion looked beautiful; she looked thinner; she acted happy.

"My mother had not had a face-lift, nor had she lost any weight (which she needed to do). A proper color change had done the trick!"

Clothes are a necessary item in our budget. We must buy them occasionally, so why not choose colors that *will do something for us.*

But why spend money going to a color analyst when there is probably a fabric shop somewhere near you? Visit it! Stand before a mirror with several bolts of material at your fingertips. Drape yourself with various colors. Does a particular color or tone of color do more than another to complement your complexion—bring out the highlight in your hair—emphasize the color of your eyes—make you look thinner or heavier? If you're in doubt, ask the opinion of someone in the store. Ask more than one! I have many times.

If you sew, which many of you do, you will have chosen a color that will make you feel special. If you must purchase your outfit, then ask for some swatches from the bolts to take shopping with you.

Specialists in the field of color have convinced me that the right colors can stimulate, motivate, and make us healthier, happier persons. Christian women need God's array of beautiful, creative colors of nature around them. The colors of the rainbow, the sky, the flowers, the grass were all made for our enjoyment—to be worn and to be used in our homes, churches, schools, hospitals. Let's not allow them to be wasted and unused.

There have been many studies made experimenting with colors in children's playrooms, classrooms, and hospitals. There has been a change in children's dispositions, moods, optimism, and energy levels according to the color of their environment. Where cheerful, warm colors were used, some children experienced a raised IQ of 12 points. It stimulated creativity and mental alertness and produced a more cheerful personality.

If colors can do this for children, perhaps we should consider doing some experimenting with ourselves.

RED is the "flame" color, the exciter!

Red is the warming element of the sun. It can have an arousing effect upon the blood and to some extent on the nerves. Consequently, it has been proven valuable to patients with paralysis and other chronic conditions.

It is one of the two most commonly preferred colors. It relates to both the introvert and the extrovert. The impulsive, possibly athletic, quick-to-speak-her-mind person may choose red. The timid and meek may choose the color because it signifies the brave qualities that she lacks.

BLUE has been called the tranquilizer and is the second best-loved color.

It is considered a conservative color and is chosen by types who have achieved, are deliberate, and seldom do anything impulsive. They often make good executives and community leaders. They often reside among other "blue lovers."

PINK is chosen more by women than men and is called the "pacifier."

Pink types are usually well-educated, indulged, and protected. They often don't have the courage to choose color in its full intensity. Pinks could signify gentility and affection. Some may choose this color because they yearn for the tenderness of pink.

ORANGE is the social color—cheerful, luminous, and warm.

It typifies the Irish character with a warm personality that gets along with everyone—rich and poor, brilliant or unlearned. Orange personalities are friendly, have a ready smile and a quick wit. They are good-natured and gregarious and love people in general.

YELLOW is the energizer.

It can be associated with the mentally and spiritually alert people. The yellow type likes innovation and originality. They tend to be discriminating and introspective.

GREEN has been called the masquerader because it is difficult to define.

Green is symbolic of nature and balance. Those who prefer green colors are invariably socially well-adjusted people. They are constantly on the move, are easy-mannered, and are not impulsive.

AQUA is considered a "fussy" color.

It is chosen mostly by people who are sophisticated, who have excellent taste, are well-dressed, sensitive, and refined.

PURPLE is the elegant color.

It's considered a royal color and looked upon as "elegant" by the average person. It may be chosen by those who are sensitive to the cultural and artistic. They may be temperamental in disposition but are usually easy to be around.

BROWN is the earthy color.

It is preferred by those who are reliable and sturdy. Brown is conservatism in the extreme! The brown type usually dislikes anything frivolous or flighty. They are often bench warmers rather than participants.

BLACK is considered a morbid color by some because people are buried in it.

It means death! However, black can be worn with elegance and is considered a "formal" color for many occasions.

WHITE is the color of purity.

Babies are dedicated in it; brides are married in it. There are more shades of white than any other color. Off-white, pearl white, Paris white, snow white, eggshell, ivory, platinum, zinc white, Chinese white, flake white, and others. Some wear it with elegance; others look washed out. Unless you have some color yourself, it's best to stay away from white unless you wear something in color with it.

Since the proper color—either worn or surrounding us—can heal, stimulate, inspire, soothe, change moods, or beautify, it's imperative that we study our world of color.

It's just as important to give attention to the wrong color. It can produce irritation, limit our attention span, cause depression, slow one down mentally, discourage motivation, and make anyone into a drab, uncolorful personality. *Let color work for you!*

SECTION IV

The Whole Woman—"Serving"

10

Fashioned for His Service

We have considered personal wholeness (body, soul, and spirit). All of this is not an end but a means to an end—serving Christ and others. For we are fashioned for His service.

There is an interesting story told about East and West Berlin during a period in history when they were anything but friendly. East Berlin, because of being dominated by the Communists, had developed a hostile spirit toward West Berlin, which was a free democracy. Giving vent to their antagonistic feelings, East Berlin took truckloads of garbage and dumped it over the boundary line into West Berlin.

Instead of retaliating, West Berlin took truckloads of canned food and nonperishable items and stacked them neatly on the borderline of East Berlin. On top of the last items was placed a large placard with these words inscribed: "Each gives what he has." This is a vivid picture of how the world sees us today!

Let's take an inventory. What kind of harvest are you and I producing? If we were trees in a fruit orchard, would the owner be pleased with what we are producing? Or would he be tempted to cut us down and replace us with healthier, more fruitful trees?

Successful service is contingent upon the level of our commitment. St. Paul sets the standard:

> "Though I am free and belong to no man,
> I make myself a slave to everyone,
> to win as many as possible."
> (1 Cor. 9:19)

This selfless devotion prepares us to fulfill our God-given mission:

> "For we are God's workmanship,
> created in Christ Jesus to do good works,
> which God prepared in advance for us to do."
> (Eph. 2:10)

Commitment To Excellence

Raphael, the famous Italian artist, was asked, "Which of your paintings is the greatest?" He said, "My next one." This was the spirit with which this gifted man excelled. It was what lifted him to the level of achievement that he enjoyed. What a dynamic vision! What high ideals! Raphael was determined never to allow stagnation to enter his painting career. He was continually reaching up, stretching, growing. When he hit one plateau, he set another one a little higher. This world-renowned artist recognized that only with persistence and determination would he realize his goals, his dreams, his aspirations.

This pattern of achievement should be one for us to follow in our Christian living today. It will mark us as uncommon, extraordinary representatives of Jesus Christ. It's the only way we will ever excel to our full potential in Christian service.

The Power of Perseverance

Abraham Lincoln, believed by many to be the greatest president of the United States, modeled the unflinching perseverance that is another key ingredient in successful service. His singleness of purpose in reaching his personal goals saw him through a succession of disappointments, rejections, and defeats. He exemplified the spirit of these timeless biblical truths:

> "If any man draw back,
> my soul shall have no pleasure in him."
> (Heb. 10:38, KJV)

> "If thou faint in the day of adversity,
> thy strength is small."
> (Prov. 24:10, KJV)

Mr. Lincoln manifested an unbelievable stamina in his political career. He had a stick-to-itiveness that finally brought him to the White House. The last key fit the lock. Look at these defeats:

1831—his business collapsed
1832—he suffered a defeat for legislature
1843—he was upset by his opponent for Congress
1848—he was defeated in his efforts for Senate
1855—he was deprived of the position of vice-president

He had stumbled. But I can almost hear Mr. Lincoln saying, "Only a worm is free from stumbling, and a worm I am not!" Lincoln was his own person. He knew who he was. He didn't leave to

God what he himself could do. He possessed a built-in motivation that refused to let him give up. This heroic man had every reason to give up in despair. But his belief in himself and a stronger, unconquerable faith in God would not allow him the option of quitting.

Although one defeat followed another, each reverse and disappointment only posed a stronger challenge and determination to prevail.

Then it happened! In 1860 Abraham Lincoln was elected the president of the United States. His faith and hope, coupled with his patience and persistence, had paid off. The slaves would be freed. The nation would be united.

But what would have happened had Abraham Lincoln—
- Become disheartened with his first defeat in 1831, 29 years prior to his presidential election.
- Not believed in himself enough to follow his dreams and goals.
- Not been willing to give himself to a cause bigger than himself—to be stretched, enlarged, challenged, disciplined.
- Failed to believe in a power higher than himself to whom he could pray for guidance, strength, and patience.

We will never know what might have been! Of this we are sure, Abraham Lincoln would never have realized his full potential and capabilities had he been a quitter, dropped by the wayside, and failed to cross the finish line in his political race.

What About You?

Am I making a correct diagnosis of your thinking right now? Are you saying, "But I can't be president!" That's right, not many can—or will. But do you have a high but achievable goal of Christian service that can be reached with the perseverance and determination so dramatically demonstrated by Lincoln? What about women like Fanny Crosby, Helen Keller, Louise Chapman, Orpha Speicher, and Mother Teresa? What about mothers who have reared children for the purpose of evangelizing the world? What about unsung women heroes who are dedicating their lives to serving others?

A friend shared this true story with me about a little-known evangelist who held a revival for a pastor who had a retarded son. The young lad, so retarded and perhaps unlovely to some, won his way into the heart of this guest speaker.

During the week of meetings the evangelist asked for the privilege of working with the child. Since the boy said only a few words, he decided this was where he would put his emphasis.

Using the five small fingers on the boy's right hand, he taught him the first five words of the 23rd psalm: "The Lord is my shepherd." Over and over again the two would start with the little finger, go to the next, then the next, and the next until he finished with his thumb as the word *shepherd.*

All week the evangelist struggled with the stammering tongue, patiently teaching the handicapped child these beautiful words.

He closed his meeting and went on his way. In about three years he returned to the same city and inquired about the boy. "Oh, he passed away," the father said. "But when he died he was holding the little finger of his right hand. He was evidently trying to repeat the scripture you had tried so hard to teach him."

For some people this gesture of love shown for a small afflicted boy might not have been an exciting mission. But to a father and son this "man of God" was being Jesus to them. No matter how small or insignificant the task, any act of kindness and mercy directed by the Lord is a special assignment.

Our Service Model

The expression that "God cannot talk with a starving man except in terms of bread" is not just making reference to physical hunger. Hurting people are crying out for help that can relate to their personal needs. Jesus became the Model for building bridges between God and humanity. Now He asks that we become builders of these bridges.

This beautiful story dramatically illustrates the example Christ set for us in this regard.

Back in the 14th century a monk announced to the people of his village that he was going to preach the greatest sermon ever preached on the love of God. He urged everyone to attend.

The day arrived. The cathedral was filled with the old and young alike. When the time came for the monk to enter the pulpit, the people waited expectantly. Finally, they saw that he was going, not to the podium, but to the tall candelabra that stood to the side of the pulpit. Lighting a long candle, he walked to the sculptured form of Christ nailed to the Cross.

Standing with his back to the congregation, he silently lifted the burning candle until the glow was directly underneath one of the pierced hands; then underneath the other. Slowly, he moved the lighted candle to the side of Jesus where the spear had pierced Him. Then, dropping to his knees in an attitude of prayer, he held the glimmering light so that the glow fell on the nail-pierced feet.

As the monk turned from the Cross to face his congregation, the candle picked up the glistening tears that trickled down from his eyes. "This, my people, is God's love message for you today."[8]

"Calvary commitment" is still the timeless standard for service.

> *Christ, if ever my footsteps should falter,*
> *And I be prepared for retreat,*
> *If desert or thorn cause lamenting,*
> *Lord, show me Thy feet—*
> *Thy bleeding feet, Thy nail-scarred feet—*
> *My Jesus, show me Thy feet!*
>
> Author unknown

My Personal Commitment

The songwriter voiced the Christian's practical commitment to service in the hymn that begins "Take my life, and let it be / Consecrated, Lord, to Thee."[9]

Let My Hands Perform His Bidding

The hand in its various aspects—physical, cultural, social, and spiritual—touches human life more vitally than any other earthly influence. No doubt this is why this valuable part of the body is honored by being used in 1,077 scripture passages—more than any other one word.

Physically, the hand is a masterpiece. Its touch is an authoritative communicator that speaks volumes. The touch of the hand affects our behavior as well as our health, according to psychological studies. From the time we are born to our last day it has the power to heal, to soothe, to comfort. By the shake of the hand you can convey love, satisfaction, approval; or you can broadcast anger, impatience, or self-consciousness.

Through the hand we enjoy a special sense of touch. For instance, Helen Keller was blind and deaf. Yet, she could "hear" by placing her fingertips on the lips of her friends. Again, by the touch of the fingers the blind can read the raised characters of the braille alphabet.

In human relationships how influential is the ministry of the hand. A clasp of the hand may be the beginning of a lifetime friendship or a lasting romance. Hands are joined at the marriage altar. They habitually open the Word of God for private and/or family devotions. A mother's comforting hand patiently guides the feet of her children and soothes a fevered brow. With the ingenious touch of a woman's hand a dwelling place becomes a home.

In the spiritual realm we pay tribute to the hands of men and women who minister the holy sacraments, who are ordained to the full-time Christian ministry, who dedicate babies and bury the dead. We commend every individual in our world today, both young and old alike, whose hands are diligently and selflessly working at the Master's business. They are an extension of the hands of Jesus. His were holy hands. Though soiled by toil, they were never soiled by sin. They were constantly employed in selfless ministry to others. An unknown author has written:

> *Lord, when I am weary with toiling,*
> *And burdensome seem Your commands,*
> *If my load should lead to complaining,*
> *Lord, show me Your hands—Your nail-pierced hands,*
> *Your cross-torn hands, my Savior, show me Your hands.*

Unlimited opportunities are open to anyone who is willing to use these wonderful instruments called hands to do service for the King. Song writer Floyd W. Hawkins captures so beautifully the purpose for which I believe God created "hands," when he wrote the song, "This Pair of Hands."

> *These hands I give to Thee, my blessed Saviour,*
> *To do Thy will whatever love demands;*
> *Redeemed and sanctified and in Thy favor,*
> *I gladly yield to Thee this pair of hands.*
>
> *To point the lost of earth to Calvary,*
> *To lift the Cross that dying souls may see,*
> *To bring Thy healing touch to darkest lands,*
> *I give to Thee, my God, this pair of hands.*
>
> —Floyd W. Hawkins

(Many of my thoughts on "Hands" were inspired by the writings of my beloved father-in-law, Ernest L. Stowe.)

Let My Feet Run in His Way

Full commitment to following the Master's service involves the use of our feet as well as our hands. Many years ago songwriter William Cushing wrote:

Ev'rywhere He leads me I would follow, follow on,
Walking in His footsteps till the crown be won. [10]

This is still the pattern of obedience that must characterize the lives of God's women today.

Where did the footsteps of Jesus go? Without exception they were involved in compassionate ministries to others.

To Children

Jesus had time to help children like the little demon-possessed daughter of the Greek woman. In response to the Mother's request He exorcised the evil spirit and made her normal again.

As *we* follow in the footsteps of our Lord, we will be led to needy boys and girls. No women's ministry is more important than that to children. It begins with our own, of course. This must be our first priority. No responsibility in the church or community is more essential. But it does not end there. Sunday School children from uncaring, non-Christian homes cry out for our tender, loving care. Our volunteer ministry to hurting children will communicate the compassion of Jesus in an unmistakable way.

To the Sick

The four Gospels are filled with stories of Jesus' compassion for suffering men and women as well as children. But He did more than sympathize with them. He healed all kinds of people of all kinds of illnesses.

We too must do more than feel sorry for hurting people. We must follow the footprints of Jesus and demonstrate Christian concern in action. For instance, thousands of elderly people in nursing homes are dying for want of a personal touch of love from people like you and me. God does not divide us into categories of age for service. When we love Christ we will witness; we will share; our feet will be busy in His way. My mother's small feet had traveled many a weary road, but in her 70s and 80s she found that they still had some mileage left.

She was on crutches as a result of surgery. Since she needed someone with her, a woman stayed in her home through the week. Then our two teenagers and I drove the 40 miles from where we lived to care for her over the weekend. The following incident left an indelible imprint on my memory.

One of the shut-ins to whom Mother ministered was very ill. Just as I was completing the preparation for Sunday dinner Mother said, "Would you please fix a tray of food for my friend.

She has no family near her and I'm concerned that she isn't eating properly."

Just as I was leaving with the food and needed directions for getting to the right house, Mother decided she wanted to go with me. So I helped her into the car—crutches and all—and we were on our way.

Mother had a key to her friend's house, so we let ourselves in. As I started toward the bedroom with the tray of food Mother said, "Faye, let me take it to her. She doesn't know you."

I'll never forget the scene. Mother laid aside her crutches, took the tray of food in her hands and, limping badly, went in to greet her friend.

The name of the recipient of the loving gesture has been forgotten, but not the one who did the loving!

The teenagers in our churches could learn many valuable lessons from ministering to elderly people. Many shut-ins have no one to give them special love and attention. How thrilled they would be to have young people come and sing to them, bring them a small gift, read to them. The youth would probably never fully realize the impact they would make on a group of hurting, lonely, discouraged, and sometimes bored people.

"But I don't have time!" Let's take a look at Jesus. Did anyone ever have more to do than He? Yet there is no record that Jesus ever got in a hurry. With all of the demands placed upon Him He could well have dashed from place to place out of breath and near panic. But He moved at a steady, patient pace with time for everyone who needed His help. When His brief life came to an end, He had completed all the work that His Father had for Him to do.

This should say something to us. What a contrast to the hurrying and fretting and fussing that have become such a vital part of so many of our lives in the 1980s. Perhaps our priorities need rearranging. If Christ had time to go and minister to the needy, shouldn't we be able to spare the time?

To the Hungry

In response to the fact that the people had nothing to eat, Jesus said, "I have compassion for these people" (Matt. 15:32). Then He proceeded to multiply seven loaves of bread and a few small fish into "dinner on the grounds!" Not only did the 4,000 have plenty to eat, but there were seven basketfuls left over to share with other hungry people.

More and more of our churches are catching the vision of feeding the hungry and clothing the needy. Pantries and spare rooms are being set up where concerned Christians may bring gifts of food and used clothing to share with the needy.

This display of love is reviving the caring spirit of Dr. P. F. Bresee, the founder of the Church of the Nazarene. He felt strongly called to preach the gospel to the poor and often neglected people of the city. The First Church of the Nazarene in Los Angeles was known for its sensitivity to the needs of the people in the community. It had a "caring center" where food and clothing were distributed daily.

This is the "heart" of evangelism, then and now. Women, we are needed to reach the heart of the lost!

On to the Cross

The footsteps of Jesus were committed to following the pathway of His Father's will for His life. In His final hours He "became obedient to death—even death on a cross!" (Phil. 2:8). And what does spiritual obedience mean to us but the willingness to have our every step directed by the Lord?

When Jesus' feet took Him into the Garden of Gethsemane, He was already feeling some of the bitterness of death. The time of suffering for Jesus was intensified by the solitude of the moment. His friends whom He had asked to stand by had fallen fast asleep.

As the shadows of the evening crept closer among the olive trees, Jesus knelt in prayer. Being yet in human form, fear gripped His heart. The fact that Jesus shrank from the final cost of His lifelong obedience to God but persevered should encourage us when we find ourselves struggling with a situation that calls for self-denial. It is comforting to know that Jesus, who walked in human flesh, understands our weaknesses, our frailties.

Not once but three times Jesus' feet took Him to the place of prayer in the Garden. Repeatedly He prayed, "Father, if you are willing, take this cup from me; yet not my will, but yours be done" (Luke 22:42).

What a lesson of obedience comes from this prayer! His submission to God's will would cost Him His very life. Jesus did not want to die any more than any strong, healthy person would. All of us love life and want to live, but like our Savior we too must bow to the Father's will in every situation, no matter what the cost.

He knew this final walk would take Him to Calvary; to the

Cross; to His death. And a commitment to follow in His footsteps of service will mean a cross for us too.

But death could not keep its prey—Jesus went on to the victory of His resurrection. And today, though absent from us physically, Jesus walks with us in the person of the Holy Spirit whom God has sent to be our Comforter and Helper.

How productive are we as His helpers? Jesus has only our feet for carrying His gospel to the unsaved. He has done His part in providing free salvation for all who will believe on the Lord Jesus Christ. But many will never know of this free gift unless it's taken to them by you and me.

His feet were pierced for us!

What are our feet giving Him in return?

Our Shadow of Influence

Wherever we walk physically we are casting a shadow. And that shadow becomes a reflection of our character and personality. Unconsciously the shadow of our influence represents one of the greatest powers we will ever possess. By it we can create an atmosphere that will speak for Christ. And *if we want to exert a good influence,* there's only one way to do it—*we must be good!*

Is the warmth of our personality and the strengthening quality of our lives lifting someone to greater heights in their spiritual walk? Do they say, "I'm a better person because of her life. She walks like Jesus walked in Spirit and in truth. Everywhere she goes she leaves behind her helpful acts of kindness. She's inspiring, encouraging"? This is the kind of life that casts a lasting influence for the Master.

In many unconscious ways we are helping to mold each personality we touch every day. This is a real revelation to some and an awesome responsibility for all of us. It's vital that we believe in people! By so doing many will make every attempt to live up to the expectations of our faith and trust in them. This should be an added incentive to so walk that we cast a shadow of trust for them to follow. When we expect nothing from people we often get nothing. The children in our homes today need to experience this shadow of influence. They need to feel our love and confidence and trust. This should encourage them to believe that they can become anything they choose to be within the will of God.

Yes, sometimes there's no need for words. The shadow of a godly walk will be all the message we need to speak for Christ.

11

Personal Beauty

A Weighty Problem

Ruby, a petite, black-haired minister's wife, shared her success story for remaining healthy without the additional strain of unnecessary pounds.

She came from a family of "overweights." Both of her sisters as well as her mother accepted the fact that they could not conquer it. They were heavy and would probably die prematurely—so what! Their attitude was devastating to Ruby. How could they not care!

Then Ruby had her first child. She, who had been so meticulous in her eating, fell into the trap of excessive nibbling. The pounds began to accumulate.

One morning following her bath. Ruby walked past a mirror and was appalled at what looked back at her. She fell on her knees beside her bed and presented her body a living sacrifice to God. She confessed her need of His counsel, His strength, His victory.

She knew if she were to prepare herself adequately for "physical battle," it would necessitate putting on the whole armor of God. With it and her trust in God she would not be defeated. When she had an urge to go on "eating binges" she would do something constructive instead. She refused to allow carelessness to become an ingrained habit that could be detrimental to her spiritual influence.

You know the answer! She won the battle! No one could possibly lose on those terms.

If today your battle is in the field of keeping your body healthy, put God to the test! He wants to perform a miracle through your body. I'm sure of it!

The expression, "It isn't what you're eating that's causing your problem but what's eating you," could largely involve one's attitude, A plastic surgeon, for instance, can give his patient a new face, but no one can give her a new attitude but herself! This is formed from her inner thoughts.

As a woman thinks in her heart, so is she.
As she continues to think, so she remains.
    Beautiful thoughts crystalize into
    spiritual habits of grace and kindness.
        Negative thoughts can control, limit,
        and eventually defeat us.

Eat properly, yes! Exercise for the sake of our general health. Set a weight that is right for us (not necessarily for anyone else). It should be one with which we can live and be at our best. Then we can forget about it! This will keep it from being a pressure point. Hopefully none of us will be tempted to experiment with fad diets. It's one sure way of damaging our health as well as upsetting our disposition.

Our Visible Witness

An attractive face and figure are not an ego trip for the woman who seeks to be fashioned in Christ's image. They are valuable "equipment" for effective service for the Master.

Through Christ we can be clothed with an inner beauty that will extend to the outside. One special speaker, after observing his audience, said, "The most important thing any of us wear is the expression on our faces. If we consistently display a sour countenance, we inevitably have sour, negative thoughts. In contrast, a cheerful countenance indicates pure, loving thoughts." The Bible substantiates this. In Prov. 15:13 we read:

"A happy heart makes the face cheerful,
but heartache crushes the spirit."

Here is a poem written by Elbert Hubbard who is also of the opinion that what we wear in our hearts is transmitted through our faces.

Upon every face is written the record of the life one has led; the prayers, the aspirations, the disappointments, all she or he hoped to be and was not, are written; nothing is hidden nor indeed can be.

A man stood in a church vestibule watching a petite, white-haired grandmother as she warmly greeted the people around her. He couldn't resist telling her how beautiful she was. She responded with a smile as she said, "I should be, I'm 78 years old! The Lord's been working on me a long time! He entrusted me with a few gifts and a strong, healthy mind and body. I've done my best to honor that trust. It has been pure joy burning out for the Lord each day, knowing that He will refuel my machinery each night. This prepares me for another day's running."

How we present ourselves to others is an important, visible witness. Good posture, for example, contributes in a major way to personal beauty. Standing, walking, and sitting correctly will bring our spines and vertebrae into proper alignment; good posture will make us more relaxed and we will feel less tired over a period of time. It will also make us look slimmer and more confident.

A Christian dress code speaks volumes to those who observe us.

> A high school senior had dressed for her date. As she came running down the stairs, her mother was visibly shaken by what she saw. Was this her innocent, God-loving daughter who had brought such joy into their home?
>
> "Ruthie, my dear," her mother said, "who are you representing tonight? Christ or Satan! Satan would like nothing better than to use an immodest dress and sexuality as a temptation to destroy two beautiful lives—yours and Jim's."
>
> Ruthie was silent, but inwardly she resented her mother's interference. Because God is continually working for our good and His glory, His timing is always perfect. Fortunately for this young lady, her date was late arriving. This gave the mother a chance to discuss the importance of avoiding all appearances of evil.
>
> Suddenly, Ruthie leaned over and gave her mother a quick hug. "When Jim arrives, please tell him I will be down very shortly." With a happy lift to her heels she ran up the stairs to dress appropriately for representing Christ.

This is a valuable illustration demonstrating that the outward appearance of a Christian reflects a cleansed mind and a pure heart. Like Ruthie, the teenager, our bodies should be clothed in proper taste and modesty of dress to accentuate the beauty of holy living. But may God forgive us, women, if we ever excuse ourselves for looking dowdy under the pretense of dressing conservatively. If we wish to have or retain the feminine identity that reflects the lovely image I believe God intended when He created woman, our appearance will always speak femininity.

Whether it be dainty undergarments, sports, tailored or formal dress, a woman's attire should make her feel good about herself. Perhaps I'm a bit old-fashioned, but I feel that it enhances our effectiveness as women if we have some feminine touch on every garment we wear. And to the feminists in our world today, may I say that I don't believe femininity will hinder any woman anywhere from succeeding in her accomplishments for Christ. Those who feel the need to compete with men need not dress, walk, sit, or act masculine. God purposefully created us as women. This makes us unique and different. Let's celebrate our specialness!

The cosmetic companies have much to say in today's world about a variety of products that are guaranteed to beautify. And what we want to believe, they make it easy to believe. Millions of dollars are spent yearly that could be used to better advantage.

Are we not to take the best possible care of our skin? Yes, of course! Just as we are responsible for the cleanliness of the body, hair, and nails. Ours is a special temple. God's Holy Spirit dwells there! But listen to what really makes us radiant and lovely. Jane Porter describes our countenance in these descriptive words:

> Her beauty is the soul shining
> through a crystalline covering.

Yes, the hand-painting of God brings a radiance and a glow from within that all cosmetic companies envy. Why? Because a "cosmetic complexion" can't compete with godly beauty. Demonstrating the fruit of the Holy Spirit can do wonders for the face. The unfading loveliness of a calm and gentle spirit is a thing very precious in the sight of God (1 Pet. 3:4).

Our appearance should verify the fact that we represent Christ to our world. The saying "You never have a second chance to make a first impression" has far deeper overtones than might appear on the surface. Everything we are or hope to accomplish for Christ is contingent on the first external impression we make before we have a chance to disclose adequately the cleansed hearts of loving and caring persons.

One day during a seminar where I was speaking, a woman raised her hand and asked this question: "Doesn't the Bible teach that God looks on the heart rather than on the outer person?" "Yes," I responded, "that's true. But, you see, God is omniscient, all-knowing. He can see into the heart. The one with whom you come in contact is only one human being looking at another. That first impression may be the one and only exposure you have as a witness for Christ to a particular individual. So you should make it a good one!"

Our outward appearance and Christian character will both be contributing factors in presenting, "wholeness in Christ" to our world today.

12

Courtesy—Love in Action

Oftentimes we find that the *greater the woman—the greater her courtesy.* And what is courtesy but another way of expressing love? When self is submerged in Christ, love will spring forth spontaneously. Have you ever considered the fact that politeness, thoughtfulness, and graciousness is a small price to pay for the respect and affection of others.

And what is love? *Love is action. Words are worthless until they are supported by action.* Many have turned away from the spoken word, but seldom have they turned away when they saw love in action. People want to see "love with skin on it." *And don't forget the magic of touch. It's a powerful way of communicating.*

Compassionate Courtesy—Through Hospitality

One of the most practical demonstrations of Christian courtesy is hospitality.

> "Share with God's people
> who are in need. Practice hospitality."
> (Rom. 12:13)
> "Offer hospitality to one another without grumbling.
> Each one should use whatever gift he has received
> to serve others, faithfully administering God's grace
> in its various forms."
> (1 Pet. 4:9-10)

Don't ever underestimate the effectiveness of your service rendered for Christ when you open your home in gracious hospitality. By so doing many have entertained angels without knowing it (Heb. 13:2).

When Jesus went about doing good and had no place to lay His head, He became a recipient of the hospitality of those with whom He had lived and taught and loved. On more than one occasion we find Christ extending this same courtesy to others in need.

Once when He had cooked fish over a fire of burning coals near where His disciples were fishing, He invited them to join Him in a breakfast of fish and bread (John 21:8-10).

Jesus had no home of His own in which to extend hospitality. But the Emmaus incident recorded in Luke 24:30-31 cast Jesus in the role of a host. He had been invited to the house of His newfound friends. It was suppertime. The *Beacon Bible Commentary* gives this interesting interpretation:

> The Stranger with whom they had offered to share their bread was the Saviour, who was . . . able to break for them the Bread of Life. This Stranger at their table suddenly became the Head of the house, the Master of the feast, and so will He be in every home and in every heart where He is invited to abide.[11]

In like manner people will recognize Jesus in us as we too break bread with our friends in our homes. All too often we entertain not the needy and hungry and lonely, but the friends with whom we have the most in common—culturally, spiritually, and intellectually. This is a very *human* thing to do and perfectly honorable. We need to associate with the people who challenge us to grow in these areas. But Jesus didn't restrict His ministry to only one class of people. He never excluded anyone from His loving concern. Each one was of equal value. It will require an unselfish love on our part to follow His example of sensitivity. But the rewards will be immeasurable! Souls will be won!

To imitate Jesus we might try mingling with those whose lives are dull; who need encouragement in their spiritual walk; who have lost their way—or have never known "the way"; couples whose relationships have lost the romantic edge; people who wait for someone to include them in a special occasion.

If Jesus was the hospitable Christ and model for us to follow, *why is hospitality not practiced more among Christian people?* There are a few reasons—and many excuses! Work schedules, small children, physical problems, a lack of money—would represent a few. But does God excuse us? May I be real honest? *Entertaining requires good hard work,* whether it be a large or small group; an informal or a sit-down dinner. It exercises our hands and feet. And some have never cared much for exercises of any description. Those unwilling to pay the price simply don't entertain—they don't bother to extend hospitality. But what a pity! These people will never know the tremendous blessings they miss. They will never know the warm feeling of reaching out to the lonely, the hurting, the socially frightened, the ones who desperately need to feel wanted and included in someone's circle of fellowship.

Let's Be Good Stewards of Our Homes!

Extend hospitality whether God has blessed us with a home that's large or small; pretentious or humble. If we wait until we have the best—or everything just right—we will wait too long. *The Lord may come soon!* Anyway, who enjoys looking at beautiful things, no matter what they are, if they look unusable or unused. That's why *it's imperative that we keep people and things in their proper perspective.* Hopefully no one would entertain in an uncleaned house or be careless with the food they prepare. But anytime things take preference over our love and concern for people, then we need to reevaluate our priorities.

If some of us allow our bodies to dictate to our minds when and what we do in opening our homes in hospitality—nothing will ever be done!

One pastor's wife expressed her attitude like this:

- Entertaining uses up too much of my energy; it devours my time; it does terrible things to my budget!
- Sometimes I complain, "But, Lord, I'm too tired today!" He whispers ever so gently, "My strength is made perfect in weakness."
- "But, Lord, my back aches! Besides, my feet and legs hurt!" He reminds me, "My yoke is light. Where did you pick up that heavy one?"
- "But, Lord, can't someone else do it? You know how full my schedule is. I simply can't spare the time."

Let's face it! Nothing worthwhile comes cheap. If entertaining is done well and effectively it will cost us something in wear and tear—and *some* money! However, there are always inexpensive menus within our budget. So let's eliminate that excuse from our list.

Large group entertaining must be planned. But don't discount the fun of spontaneous get-togethers. I love them!!

We *should entertain with such exquisite simplicity* that no one will ever feel uncomfortable, regardless of her status in life. Our purpose is to have a good time ourselves; then we put everyone else at ease. Enthusiasm and laughter and fun are contagious! Let's be an example for Jesus. Let's infect others! Few people have ideas that originate with themselves. Most of them germinated from someone else's seed of thought.

It's disturbing to me when I hear a woman say, "All I can do is mop floors and do dishes." Now that's good as far as it goes. No one enjoys a clean, tidy home more than I. And unless we have maid service we will all at some time during the day find these mundane things staring us in the face. But being a good homemaker is an art within itself. There are fantastic opportunities to exert one's personal creativity. Since the home often takes on the personality of the individual, this should be an added incentive for working hard to make our homes a special place to share.

For example, consider the tone of your home. It will speak of warmth, joy, and harmony, or it will reflect indifference, unhappiness, and turmoil.

The *proper color tones* can transform the moods of the individuals living in your home. You will discover that color schemes will lend warmth and cheerfulness or can be depressing, bleak, and melancholy.

Lighter colors, like mirrored walls, have a tendency to push out the walls of your home a few feet. This will give a feeling of spaciousness. People don't mind being crowded; they just don't like *feeling* crowded. There is a difference!

Our home should have an atmosphere that soothes and uplifts. A gentle hostess never loses her poise and self-control, regardless! By possessing a sense of humor and some good common judgment she can never be thrown off-balance by anyone.

What about those unexpected drop-in guests? What would Jesus do? He would make them feel loved, wanted, and welcomed. We do the same!

Any home gathering *may* offer a wonderful opportunity for giving some object lesson in gracious behavior. If something is spilled on a divan or mud is tracked in on a light carpet, it's essential that we never cause that guest to feel uncomfortable. The divan or carpet can be cleaned. If not, they are only things of material value that can be replaced—friends cannot!

When my husband and I were serving at the seminary, I spoke to a group of parsonettes on the subject, "Serving Through Hospitality." One rather quiet but sincere student cornered me after the session and asked me this question, "Do you have to be born with poise and warmth and graciousness, or can you develop it?" I knew the home from which she had come. There had been very little warmth and love demonstrated in her family. I tried to assure her that what she really wanted to be she could be—providing she wanted it badly enough. God waits to help us mature and develop in any area of our personality where there's an obvious lack. He is continually molding us in His image—remember!

13

Creative Hospitality

The Home

There is no substitute for cleanliness. Whether a home is plain or elegant, large or small—a tidy, well-kept home filled with a large portion of love, unselfishness, and understanding is a delight to visit.

Two Basic Keys to Successful Entertaining

1. *Proper preparation:* Everything possible should be gotten out of the way the day before you entertain. Linens, dishes, silverware, and serving pieces should all be checked.

Salads, desserts, and even some hot dishes can be prepared in advance and refrigerated until time to cook or heat for your meal.

2. *Allow time for emergencies:* In planning for any gathering in your home it's wise to allow some extra time for unexpected delays and interruptions. You will be more relaxed and ready to enjoy your guests.

What and How to Serve

Keep the menu simple but attractive and tasty. This will free us to be with our guests. I feel badly when I am entertained in a lovely home where exotic food is beautifully served to a dinner party, but the hostess never sits down at the table.

Although we may need to get up from the table a few times, don't you feel our guests are more comfortable if we occupy the chair of the hostess? (A large group of 20 to 40 is a different story. Someone must be on her feet to keep things running smoothly. However, we can still mingle with our guests—visiting and even suggesting topics for discussion, etc.)

Unless we have someone helping in the kitchen it's often easier to serve buffet style anytime the number of guests reaches over 10 people. It becomes difficult to do our own serving without being absent too much from the table.

There are some of our friends who panic at the thought of entertaining in their home—whether it's a large or smaller group. Yet, they are elated when we include them in our party. If they are sincere in offering to help us, let's allow them to do so. They will feel less guilty not reciprocating.

Be Creative. Use some initiative! Be experimental!

No friend appreciates your borrowing all of her choice recipes and serving them to the same group of people she entertains. Find your own. Keep your eyes open for unusual recipes for different occasions. If you don't care for a recipe as it is—change it! Add to it! Omit something you don't like. In other words, make it your own.

Do you serve either a hot or cold drink to your guests as they arrive? I have found that it gives them something with which to occupy their time until the other guests arrive. Personally, I seldom suggest that our guests be seated immediately when they arrive at our home. Many prefer walking around with their cups or glasses in their hands while looking at our home or visiting with other guests.

Avoid serving meals that are too heavy. The average person today is eating less meat and more fresh fruits and vegetables. We should be as thoughtful of our guests as we are in planning for our own daily menu. Let's not encourage them to eat anything but the best in healthy foods. If dessert is served, it should be something light—especially if we're serving a full-course meal.

If *we're serving food later in the evening,* something easily digested is recommended. It will be to our advantage. No hostess enjoys hearing that her guests have gone home from her party to toss and turn, unable to sleep.

Let's Get Away from the Traditional

1. *A One-home Progressive Dinner.* It's a great way to become better acquainted. And there's no need to travel from house to house.

Use a patio or veranda; a family room, dining or living room. If it's needed, even a bedroom can be made to serve us in promoting this idea.

We set up tables according to the space we have in each room.

Number each table. For the first course, each table will have a place card for each guest. This card will indicate where they will sit at each succeeding course.

Appetizer	Main entree
Salad	Dessert

After dinner tea, Sanka, or cold drinks

2. *Come as a Native.* Invite each guest to bring a favorite dish representing his or her native state or country.

If possible, allow time for the sharing of information concerning the various dishes—where they originated, why a particular recipe was chosen as their favorite, etc. It often leads into discussions of parental influences during their formative years.

I guarantee you will close the evening feeling closer to the individuals you've entertained in your home.

3. *A Costume Party* can be dramatic and exciting providing your guests choose costumes that have significant meaning.

Biblical characters

Famous authors

Popular political personalities

Pair examples: Romeo and Juliet

Anthony and Cleopatra

Butler and maid

(The encyclopedia will help you discover some clever and hilarious things as a couple or individual.)

Plan to give prizes for the most authentic and funniest costumes. Some people who are timid about speaking or performing may be completely relaxed about coming as *they aren't!*

4. *A Fun Evening of Music.* Have the musicians bring their favorite instrument or at least something with which they can keep time to music. Form an impromptu orchestra and play familiar songs. Or you may invite vocal musicians and form a small singing group.

Again, let's add interest by finding out why they chose a particular instrument; at what age they began their lessons; if there are famous musicians in their families.

Since our guests will be limited to those who have musical ability, choosing a musician to assist you is a help.

5. *A Valentine Party.* If you are as sentimental as I am, keeping romance alive and well is vital.

Make this occasion a time of reminiscing about former days with your husband or wife, sweetheart or special friend. Here again, involving the guests in our party plans will *make it a success!*

If couples or friends have kept their first valentine, pictures, or letters from courtship days or have wedding pictures, encourage them to share.

Have a few questions at your fingertips:

- Qualities that attracted you to your mate or friend.
- Special miracles of God's grace that the two of you have experienced together.
- Events or circumstances that have been influential in molding your lives more closely together in Christian and marital love.

This could easily be a time of heart-searching for a couple who may have allowed the fires of romance to burn a little low in their marriage. Perhaps someone's testimony could turn the tide in a couple's relationship. We never know when seed is going to fall on fertile soil.

Having the couples join hands while you pray together as a group would be an effective way to close your evening.

6. *An International Dinner* could well be the most profitable evening we've ever spent entertaining. It could be enlightening as well as opening up a brand-new world of needs and prayer burdens.

The special guest list could include:

Missionaries or families of missionaries

People of different nationalities in our neighborhood

Members in the congregation
who specialize in fixing international food

When extending the invitation, deciding who will represent which country is important. They may choose to come in their native dress.

Have each guest prepare a *"sentence"* report on a missionary from the country he represents. If there are neighbors or outsiders (hopefully there will be), perhaps the hostess could choose a representative from that country for them.

At various times during the evening pause for a moment of prayer for one of the missionaries. *Christ an unseen Guest at every gathering!* This is our primary goal.

129

7. *A Sunday-evening Brunch* can be a delight!
What do you like?

- Breakfast steak with candied apples, whole wheat muffins, hash potatoes, fresh fruit cup
- Canadian bacon, scrambled eggs, date-loaf bread, a piece of fresh fruit, fruit juice
- Your favorite omelet with all those goodies added, crisp bacon and a piece of your favorite fruit
- Special blueberry pancakes or waffles topped with fresh strawberries and whipped cream, ham or bacon
- Some may prefer grapefruit made into baskets with handles (very easily done) filled with fresh fruit and topped with a mint leaf. This is good with French toast and crisp bacon.

Serve a hot drink and enjoy yourselves.

8. *A Work and Witness Party* is an evening of togetherness.

Select older couples who need their houses painted, their yards groomed, etc. Our summer evenings are long. With a number of men and women working, a few hours of fun could transform some older people's homes.

You will get hungry, so be sure and plan adequate food to feed your party of volunteers.

You will be blessed, your recipients will be overwhelmed—and think of the smile you'll bring to the face of Jesus.

(Don't forget the single adults! So often we only include couples. There are 60 million singles in America today. Whether they are Christians or not, many are hungry for friendship and fellowship.)

9. *The "Open Heart" of Christmas*
Your invited guests will gather to prepare the gifts, then go out to "play Santa."

- Locate one to five needy families to whom you may demonstrate "love in action."
- Find out the ages of the children and size of clothing they wear. Do the same for the parents.
- Give your closet a "face lift" by relieving it of some excess baggage you're not using. *Good* used clothing is very acceptable to needy families.
- Assign each woman guest a piece of new clothing to purchase, indicating sex and size. Have the men (if they will) buy toys

for the children. Have each one bring several items of food. A "food pounding" is always a fun thing to do.

- Perhaps the women would enjoy meeting together early and wrapping the gifts and new clothing. "Togetherness" is always more stimulating.

- Some could bring Bibles. Someone may have a new one at home they aren't using. These will be presented to each family, followed by prayer. I would suggest that you mark some special Bible references on the front or back page of the Bible that direct people to the Lord. You will know whether or not they are Christians.

- The group can all go together or divide into smaller numbers:
  —sing two or three Christmas carols outside the home
  —present your gifts
  —when presenting the Bible someone may choose to give the Christmas story in a "capsule." Then pray with the family. If they don't attend church, invite them to yours.

Food: You will have had your soul nourished and your "open heart" blessed. Now you feed the physical! Keep it simple.

If your crowd is large, you may want to make it very informal and have a "serve yourself" menu.

Chili, pizza, tacos, spaghetti
Tossed salad and fresh fruit
Hot drinks

Creative hospitality—a loving gesture and an exciting witness for Christ!

14

Saved to Serve

Jesus demonstrated immortal love when He looked up into the face of God, then down into the face of man in a sacrificial, selfless, noble act of divine love. Love—an immortal virtue so great that only God could design it.

- Christ didn't just talk about love; He exercised it in word and deed.

- Our Savior didn't merely talk about forgiveness; He demonstrated it. "Father, forgive them; for they know not what they do" (Luke 23:34, KJV).

- Our Master didn't only talk about "His power to save"; His life exemplified it.

And if we are really saved, we will do more than just talk to other Christians about His love, forgiveness, and power to save. We will demonstrate it. In his beautiful gospel song, Bill Gaither expresses the sentiments of his heart in speaking of serving God because we love Him. That's the primary motivation for "salvation service." We will love the unlovely and point them to Jesus because He first loved us. We will share our faith because He gave His life to save us—and them.

Just Jesus and You

Try to picture in your imagination my husband and me walking down the sidewalk in the busy city of Chicago. Suddenly I recognize Nancy, a close friend from high school days, coming toward us. In my enthusiasm, I leave the side of my husband to embrace her. Then we proceed to walk off together chatting and laughing, without one backward look or any thought of my husband who has never met Nancy. He stands alone, unrecognized, noticeably embarrassed and humiliated. I had told him repeatedly how much I loved and respected him—but I was unwilling to introduce him to my friend.

You say, "That's foolish! No one would be so rude and un-caring!" You are right, of course. No one would be! Not if she really loved and respected her husband. Yet, how many times have we been guilty of just such an act in our relationship with the One whom we say we love with all of our hearts. Jesus Christ stands by waiting to be introduced to someone who has never met Him. And we walk away completely oblivious and insensitive to His presence.

Does Jesus not have every right to question the sincerity of our love for Him? He gives us an opportunity to witness time and time again—and we completely "blow" it! Lost souls who might have been lifted to an unfailing faith in Christ are left to grope on in their sin, in utter despair and hopelessness. Just as the Master opened blind eyes in Galilee, He waits to open our eyes so that we can see harvest fields of human need at our doorsteps.

The failure to express love at the exact moment God speaks can be so crucial. It can actually jeopardize someone's eternal life. It's possible to cut off God's opportunity to draw someone to himself at a time when an individual needs Him the most.

Ours is to love and to share; His is to save and to transform. As Reuben Welch says, "We really do need each other." Not only in the realm of personal relationships, but also in the heavenly-human re-lationship between Christ and His followers. *And to whom are we to go?* To the rich and poor; the young and old; the great and small! Does it really matter? It didn't to Jesus and it must not to us! All are equally valuable to Him and we are to see them through His eyes. He said, "Whatever you did for one of the least of these . . . you did for me" (Matt. 25:40).

> *Christ claims our help in many a strange disguise*
> *Now bed-ridden, on a bed He lies;*
> *Homeless He wanders—now beneath the stars;*
> *Now count the number of His prison bars;*
> *Now bends beside us, crowned with hoary hairs.*
> *No need to climb the heavenly stairs,*
> *And press our kisses on His feet and hands;*
> *In every one who suffers,*
> *He, the man of sorrows stands!*
>
> Author unknown

A good life will sow love. It will raise a harvest of righteousness. "You did not choose me, but I chose you to go and bear fruit—fruit that will last" (John 15:16).

The greatest reward that any of us may receive will be when someone whose life we have touched will say of us—

> Because of her quiet spirit I know Christ.
> She loved everyone with a godly love.
> She was never too busy to listen, to pray, to give.
> She always made me want to be a better person.

You may not be a miracle worker in the eyes of others, but if you reflect His love and His grace, you will leave behind you the image of Christ in the lives of others. That is the greatest miracle of all! That is the greatest contribution of the *Whole Woman— Fashioned in His Image!*

Footnotes

SECTION I

1. Jo Petty, comp., *Apples of Gold* (Norwalk, Conn. : C. R. Gibson Co., 1962), 55.
2. E. Stanley Jones, *Mastery* (Nashville: Abingdon Press, 1955), 97.
3. J. Oswald Sanders, *Spiritual Leadership* (Chicago: Moody Press, 1967), 76.
4. Arthur and Nancy DeMoss, eds., *Family Album* (Valley Forge, Pa. : Family Album Publications, 1972), material paraphrased from story in this work.
5. Mary D. James, "All for Jesus," *Worship in Song* (Kansas City: Lillenas Publishing Co., 1972), 291.
6. Henry Wadsworth Longfellow, "Driftwood," in *Flowers That Never Fade* by Leroy Brownlow (Fort Worth: Brownlow's Pub. Co., 1959), 10.

SECTION II

7. Oswald Chambers, *Shade of His Hand* (Port Washington, Pa. : Christian Literature Crusade, 1973), 57.

SECTION IV

8. Walter B. Knight, comp., *Knight's Treasury of Illustrations* (Grand Rapids: William B. Eerdmans Pub. Co., 1963), material paraphrased from story in this work.
9. Frances R. Havergal, "Take My Life, and Let It Be," *Worship in Song* (Kansas City: Lillenas Publishing Co., 1972), 281.
10. William O. Cushing, "Follow On," *Worship in Song* (Kansas City: Lillenas Publishing Co., 1972), 328.
11. Charles L. Childers, *Luke, Beacon Bible Commentary* (Kansas City: Beacon Hill Press of Kansas City, 1964), 6:614.